150 Best New Eco Home Ideas

150 Best New Eco Home Ideas

Francesc Zamora Mola

HARPER
DESIGN

An Imprint of HarperCollins Publishers

HarperCollins books may be purchased for educational, business, or sales promotional use.
For information, please email Special Markets Department at SPsales@harpercollins.com.

First published in 2017 by:
Harper Design
An Imprint of HarperCollins*Publishers*
195 Broadway
New York, NY 10007
Tel.: (212) 207-7000
Fax: (855) 746-6023
harperdesign@harpercollins.com
www.hc.com

Distributed throughout the world by:
HarperCollins*Publishers*
195 Broadway
New York, NY 10007

Editorial coordinator: Claudia Martínez Alonso
Art director: Mireia Casanovas Soley
Editor and texts: Francesc Zamora Mola
Layout: Cristina Simó Perales

ISBN 978-0-06-256909-7

Library of Congress Control Number: 2016958633

Printed in China
First printing, 2017

CONTENTS

INTRODUCTION

Eco-friendly and sustainable design, LEED-certification, and *carbon footprint* are terms that have become prevalent in contemporary architecture, which has been evolving toward a more environmentally conscious practice. In some cases, this evolution has been encouraged by government regulations in an effort to reduce the negative impact of construction on the environment. Diminishing natural resources, pollution, and climate change are among the consequences of indiscriminate building policies, which affect not only the environment but also the economy and public health. Adhering to sustainable methods in the planning of a house can provide healthy, beneficial results for the occupants.

The minimization of energy consumption and maximization of energy efficiency, the reuse of salvaged construction materials, and the incorporation of ancestral style building methods offer a wide array of design opportunities, balancing environmental, economic, and societal goals.

Before we approach the concept of eco-friendly and sustainable architecture, and point out representative examples, we need to understand the ramifications of the carbon footprint. Basically, this term refers to a building's CO_2 emissions. We also need to understand that electrical energy generated through fossil fuels—such as crude oil, natural gas, and coal—is the cause of enormous amounts of CO_2 emissions.

One would think that reducing the consumption of electricity would mitigate the problem, and reasonably so. But how would we go about heating and cooling our homes? How would we light them up at night? And how would we power our kitchen appliances?

The projects featured in this book demonstrate that renewable energy—mainly from the sun and wind—is an attractive alternative for those of us, who don't mind going a little out of our way to improve the environment. That means not only minimizing fossil fuel energy consumption but also maximizing energy efficiency. The goal is to minimize the use of high energy-consuming devices.

The location, orientation, and layout of a house—open plan and courtyard house typology—are key to achieving this goal. Passive design principles make the most of sun exposure, natural ventilation, thermal mass, and glazing, contributing to thermal comfort.

When it comes to conserving natural resources, there are also many opportunities to ensure sustainable practices through the reuse of salvaged construction materials and demolition waste. The benefits of reusing waste are considerable. For instance, in the production of concrete, a large percentage of natural aggregate can be replaced with recycled waste. This would reduce the use of a nonrenewable resource, the destruction of natural habitats, and the emission of air pollutants.

With construction methods moving in a more sustainable direction, we observe a symbiosis of nature and architecture. For example, some structures demonstrate how ancestral vernacular design solutions—such as the earth-bermed house—can be used in contemporary architecture in combination with current technologies.

All these new design principles are changing the way we plan, build, and operate our homes. Balancing aesthetic and environmental measures can, in most cases, result in important economic savings over the lifetime of a home, but even more important, provide beneficial results aimed at the creation of healthy and pleasant homes.

Tucson Mountain Retreat

DUST

Tucson, Arizona, United States
© Jeff Goldberg/Esto

This rammed-earth dwelling is located in an arid expanse of land that emits a sense of stillness and permanence. It holds mysteries of magical proportions. The home is carefully sited in response to the adjacent arroyos, rock outcroppings, ancient cacti, animal migration paths, air movement, sun exposure, and views. Great effort was invested to minimize the physical impact of the home in such a fragile environment. Rooted in the desert, where water is always scarce, the design incorporates a generous 30,000-gallon rainwater harvesting system with an advanced filtration device that produces the most precious resource available for all household uses.

Parking is intentionally isolated from the house. From there, one must walk along a narrow footpath, passing through a dense clustered area of cacti and Palo Verde that obscures direct views of the home. Upon each progressive footstep, the house slowly reveals itself, as if rising out of the ground.

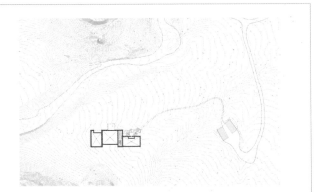

Site plan

The program of the home is divided into three distinct and isolated zones: living, sleeping, and music recording/home entertainment. Each zone can only be accessed by stepping outside. This separation resolves the clients' desired acoustic separation, while offering an opportunity for continual experiencing the desert landscape.

Roof deck plan

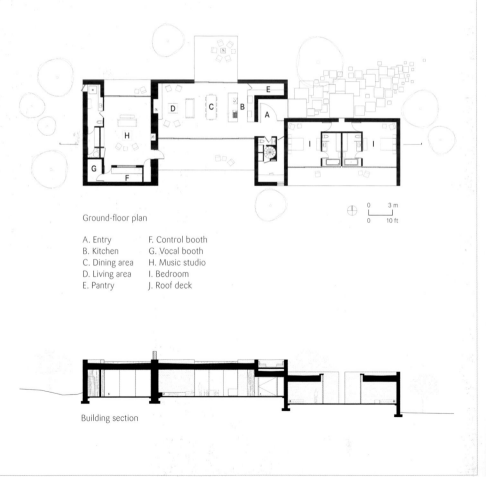

Ground-floor plan

A. Entry
B. Kitchen
C. Dining area
D. Living area
E. Pantry

F. Control booth
G. Vocal booth
H. Music studio
I. Bedroom
J. Roof deck

Building section

001

The entry sequence, a series of playfully engaging concrete steps, dissolves into the desert, merging nature and construction.

002

The main living area and the sleeping spaces extend into south-facing patios that offer views and access to the Sonoran Desert. Deep overhangs provide shelter from the high summer sun, while allowing low winter sunlight to passively heat the interior.

003

Climatic conditions must drive the architecture, including form, layout, type of construction, and details, in order to achieve comfortable living spaces.

004

Solar heat gain is reduced by orienting the house in a linear fashion along an east-west axis, and by minimizing door and window openings in the narrow east and west facades, creating comfortable spaces where light and temperature can be controlled.

A perforated steel staircase leads to the roof terrace. The space that contains it is dark and boasts a mysterious atmosphere that encourages contemplation. The harsh desert light from above filters through the perforated steel, as if slowly consuming it.

Nook Residence

MU Architecture

Mansonville, Québec, Canada
© Ulysse Lemerise Bouchard
via ww.v2com-newswire.com

The Nook Residence appears like an origami structure, clinging to the steep terrain where it sits and projecting toward a nearby lake. Despite its unassuming front façade, large openings that pierce the entire house encourage exploration. They offer peeks of the landscape beyond and ease the integration of the house into its surrounding natural landscape.

The façades bend in and out, creating protected outdoor spaces while directing the views from all the interior spaces toward different angles. Acting as a landmark through the lush summer, the house changes with the seasons, and its whiteness blends into the winter landscape as a tribute to the great Québec winters.

Horizontal siding painted white
covers all exterior walls and allows
a delicate integration of the building
into its environment.

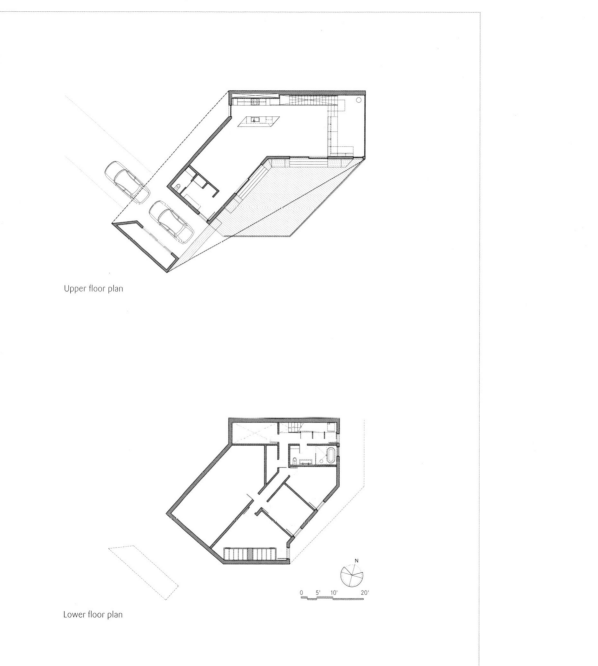

Upper floor plan

Lower floor plan

N

0   5'   10'   20'

005

Cedar ceilings extend to the roof soffits outside, stretching sights to the lake. Cedar is considered a very sustainable building product, coming from a renewable resource and producing low amounts of greenhouse gases.

006

The use of high-quality materials ensures that the house meets durability expectations and preserves its visual appeal through its lifetime. Maintenance requirements is another factor that is often taken into account in sustainable building.

A sitting area three steps below the main living area comes as a pause in the architectural adventure. This area, which promotes relaxation and contemplation, accentuates the appreciation of the site.

The sobriety of materials creates a canvas for a space that is both bright and warm. Polished concrete radiant floors, black ceramic tiles, and walnut furniture complete the interiors in a well-balanced composition dominated by clean lines.

House in the Woods

Officina29 Architetti

Sardinia, Italy

© Joao Morgado

The powerful presence of oak trees and the sloping terrain guided the design of this house. The scale of the building was kept to a minimum, so as not to compete with the grandeur of the surrounding trees. To make the most of the limited space, furniture was custom-made. Each natural element was respected; not one tree was cut down to make room for the house. The reinforced concrete pillars support the structure above the ground. This building is actually an annex to an existing house nearby. The native understory was preserved and enhanced through interesting and complex vegetation combinations, easy to maintain and suitable for a shady environment.

007

Excessive disruption of the understory can destroy a natural habitat. The area of a site that is being developed needs to be restored immediately to avoid the displacement of native wildlife and to prevent erosion.

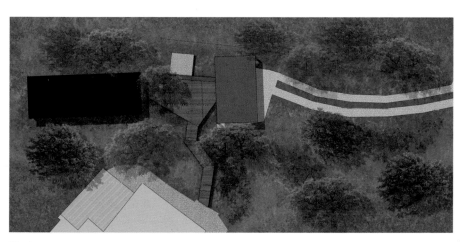

Site plan

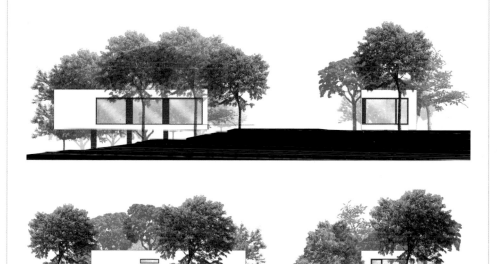

Building elevations

008

House in the Woods is a straightforward orthogonal volume elevated off the ground to minimize site impact. Raising a building also avoids easy access to certain pests and prevents flooding in regions that are vulnerable to it.

A wooden path, made of overlapping platforms, negotiates around the trees and clumps of vegetation between the existing house and the new structure, offering a spatial experience that promotes contemplation.

009

The building has large glazed openings that create an unobtrusive building envelope, allowing the building to merge with its surroundings, hence minimizing visual impact.

The interior space is equipped with a wall kitchen, a bathroom, and a sleeping area. It is therefore independent from the main residence nearby. Its versatile character offers various usage options.

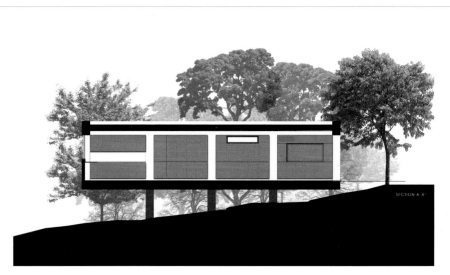

Building section A

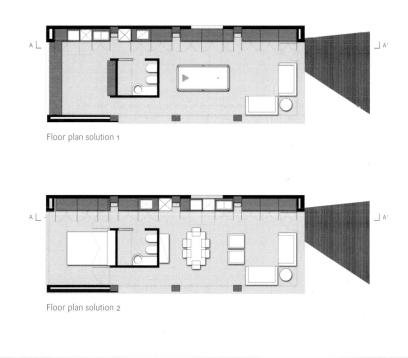

Floor plan solution 1

Floor plan solution 2

Because of its location in a densely forested area, the building is virtually in the shade. This is particularly convenient for the summer. In the winter, when the trees have lost their leaves, light reaches the building to warm up its interior.

011

The bathroom is the only actual room in the building. It acts as organizer of the space, which is completely open, to allow a flexible use.

The partitions that enclose the bathroom are short of the ceiling to highlight the general proportions of the building and maintain an open feel.

This small dwelling provides its occupant with a retreat to call home for short stays, as well as an art studio in which to work in a quiet environment. The retreat, carefully nestled among tall trees, enjoys views that stretch from the tree crowns and dark mossy undergrowth to long vistas of the Pacific Ocean. The client's wishes for simplicity in program, gentle exterior appearance, small footprint, and abundant natural light set the guidelines for an open sculptural form. Great effort was put into minimizing the building's impact on the site, resulting in a long, yet slim, structure.

Rain Forest Retreat

AGATHOM Co.

Vancouver Island,
British Columbia, Canada

© Steve Evans

012

Being set in the shade of the tall trees, all that was required for cooling were carefully chosen operable windows at low and high reaches, creating constant and natural fresh air movement.

The main art studio is set against the poetic stand of slim but towering Douglas fir trees, framed by a 14-foot-high window. In contrast, a low, horizontal picture window celebrates the darkness and damp mosses of the forest floor. The juxtaposition of these views engages the fine detail of immediate foreground with the power of the larger rain forest setting.

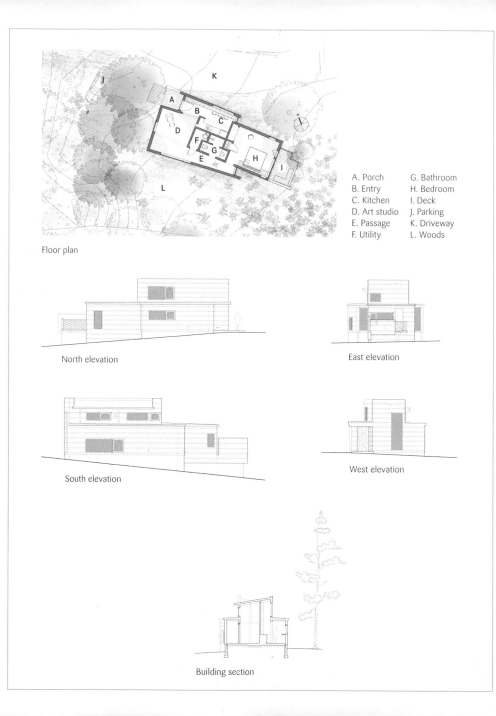

Floor plan

A. Porch   G. Bathroom
B. Entry   H. Bedroom
C. Kitchen   I. Deck
D. Art studio   J. Parking
E. Passage   K. Driveway
F. Utility   L. Woods

North elevation

East elevation

South elevation

West elevation

Building section

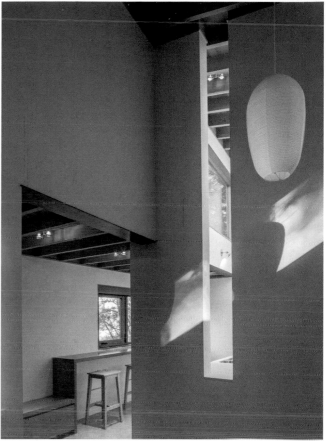

By slightly twisting two main blocks of the plan, and overlapping these shapes, a building modest in area is ever expansive and full of unexpected depth. Spaces overlap and reveal themselves gradually as one moves through the house.

The use of local red cedar on the exterior and local Douglas fir in the interior reflects the traditional timber building style of the region. The lumber for the project was locally milled to project-specific sectional profiles that provide warmth, distinction, and high quality.

The structural roof members were carefully planned and exposed, an homage to the dwelling's natural environment. The millwork and windows were also crafted from local fir, completing a full set of ingredients sourced and prepared from within a short radius of the project.

Settling on the floor plan was an
exercise in developing a program that
demanded flexibility. This effort went
hand in hand with the desire to create a
peaceful creative retreat that embraced
the natural sensory gifts of the site.

Carefully sited clerestory windows throughout the home's upper ceilings allow interior views to reach treetops, adding a great sense of expanse, unexpected canopy views, and dazzling light.

Edgeland House

Bercy Chen Studio

Austin, Texas, United States

© Paul Bardagjy

Edgeland House is located on a rehabilitated brownfield site. It is a modern reinterpretation of one of the oldest housing typologies in North America, the Native American pit-house. The pit-house, typically sunken, takes advantage of the earth's mass to maintain thermal comfort throughout the year. Such an architectural setting presents an opportunity for maximum energy efficiency. This project sets new standards for sustainability, while providing great aesthetic qualities through its small footprint and integrated mechanical features.

Lady Bird Johnson Wildflower Center collaborated with the reintroduction of more than forty native species of plants and wildflowers to the Edgeland House green roof and site, serving to help protect the local ecosystem.

FALL

WINTER

SPRING

SUMMER

Seasonal diagram of native wildflowers

TEXAS LANTANA

MEXICAN HAT

TROMPETILLA

TULIPAN DEL MONTE

TEXAS BLUEBONNET

WIDOW'S TEARS

BUSH PEA

DAMIANTITA

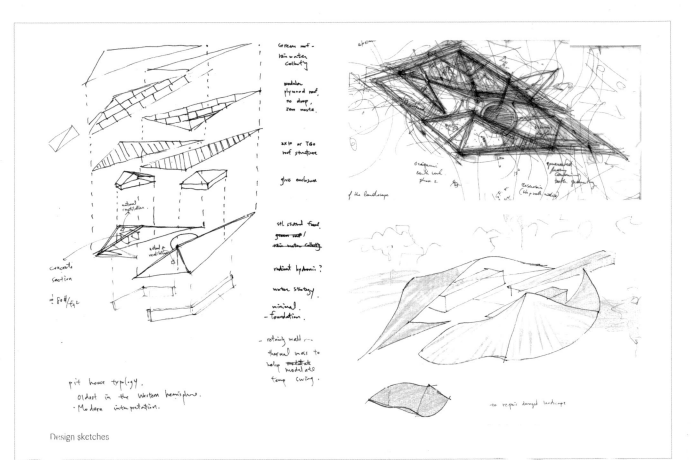

Design sketches

Both visually and functionally, Edgeland House touches on architecture as site-specific installation art and as an extension of the landscape.

Currently running down the center of the site is an abandoned Exxon pipeline, which will be excavated and removed.

An existing brownfield site contains a decommissioned oil pipeline that once belonged to Exxon.

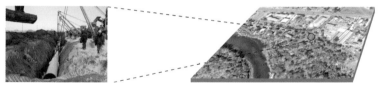

AFTER This science-fiction writer's retreat is the healing of the land; a charged site where the urban/industrial condition once met nature in a brutal and unsympathetic manner.

Pipeline diagram

Building section 1

Building section 2

013

The project raises awareness of a diminishing natural landscape and its finite resources by creating a balance between the surrounding industrial zone and the natural river residing on the opposite side of the site.

The program is broken up into two separate pavilions, one for daytime activities, the other for resting. With no enclosed passage between the two blocks, going from one to the other requires direct contact with the outside elements.

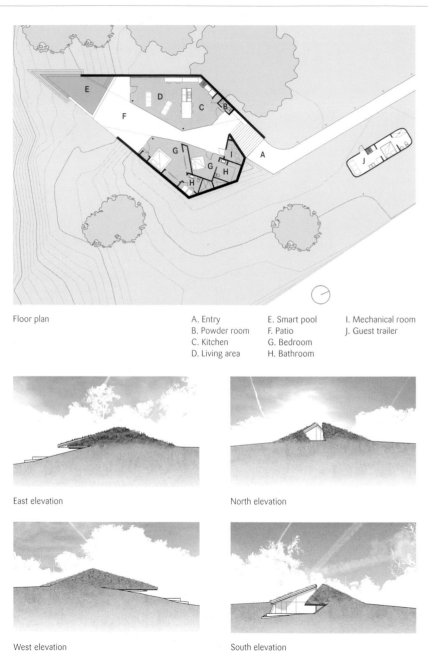

Floor plan

A. Entry
B. Powder room
C. Kitchen
D. Living area
E. Smart pool
F. Patio
G. Bedroom
H. Bathroom
I. Mechanical room
J. Guest trailer

East elevation

North elevation

West elevation

South elevation

Edgeland House's relationship to the landscape, in terms of building performance, involves an insulative green roof and a 7-foot excavation that takes advantage of the earth's thermal mass to keep the house cool in the summer and warm in the winter.

015

Glazing technologies are continuallly improving to strengthen glass's position as an indispensable building material. Modulating solar heat and light transmission, as well as improving its thermal insulation performance, are two principal goals.

As a result of these improvements, it is fair to say that efficient glazing solutions contribute to the creation of modern, comfortable, and low-energy constructions.

This project is an example of how vernacular constructions can provide sustainable solutions to contemporary designs, and how modern technologies can adapt traditional building styles to contemporary needs.

Kentfield Residence

**Turnbull Grifin Haesloop
Architects**

Kentfield, California,
United States

© David Wakely Photography

The topography of a steep site and the views it offered played a key role in determining the design of this house. Positioned to engage the surrounding landscape, the construction features a curved retaining wall that follows the contours of the hillside, anchoring the house to the steep site. To maximize contact with nature, the house is tucked under a living roof. In order to reduce its impact on the environment, the house features eco-friendly solutions, including passive and active heating and cooling systems, battery storage, and a cistern for water-runoff management.

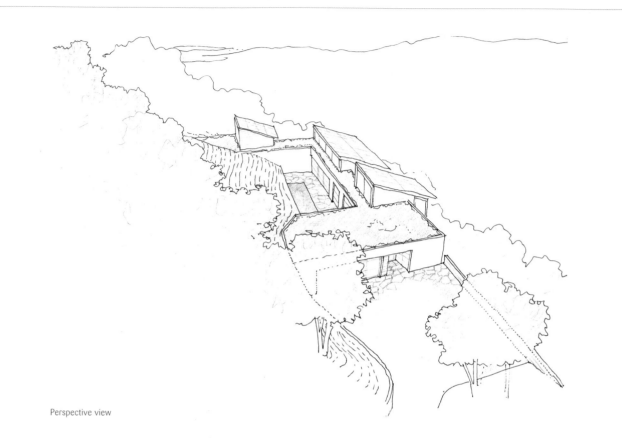

Perspective view

018

Three volumes housing the living room, kitchen-dining area, and master bedroom rise above the living roof, with shed roofs angled to capture the sun for photovoltaic and solar hot-water panels.

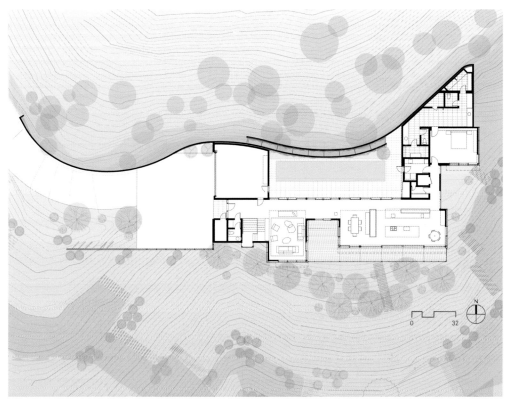

Floor plan

019

Environmental concerns are a key driver behind sustainable design. Incorporating sustainable principles in a design can lower the impact on ecosystems and the use of natural resources, as well as reducing waste production and the emission of air pollutants.

In order to minimize visual impact, the house is built against a hillside, with a retaining wall following the contour of the topography. Earth is bermed on top of the lower floor, merging with the surrounding landscape.

An interior courtyard wedged between
the house and the retaining wall offers
a secluded outdoor space for a pool,
protected from wind drafts.

020

Water, like wood or sun energy, is a resource. In view of this, the plant selection not only should respond to the preservation of native species but also allow for the reduction of water use for irrigation.

021

Clerestory roofs can improve
the lighting quality of an
interior space. Light that
passes through a clerestory
window is reflected by the
sloped ceiling—preferably
a light color—then diffused
evenly.

022

Clerestory roofs also facilitate cross ventilation, creating an air path between openings up high, close to the ceiling, and lower ones on the opposite side. This helps to displace the hot air that tends to collect near the ceiling.

Glazed openings in various walls of a room balance out lighting, achieving visual comfort. On the other hand, skylights offer architectural flexibility in rooms where windows can infringe on privacy, while still ensuring that these rooms are predominantly lit by natural light.

Earthwall 2

Ward + Blake Architects

Squirrel, Idaho, United States

© Roger Wade

Earthwall 2 deserves recognition for its sensitivity to the site, low-maintenance materials, and sustainability. This single-story house is carefully sited to minimize its environmental impact. It is set low to blend into the horizontal landscape. Rammed-earth walls and sod roofs reinforce the connection with the natural surroundings, while contributing to sustainability with their inherent insulation properties, which make this house a very energy-efficient construction. At the same time, these two distinctive construction techniques give the house a strong identity tied to vernacular.

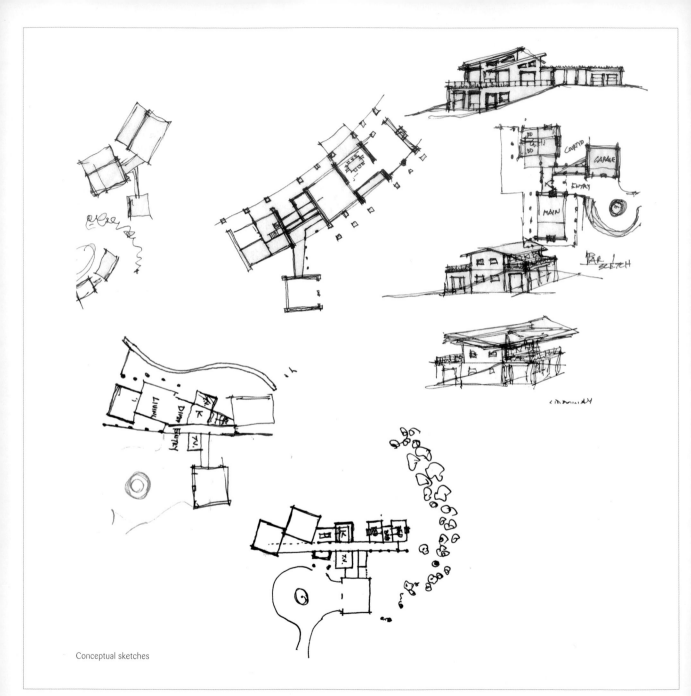

Conceptual sketches

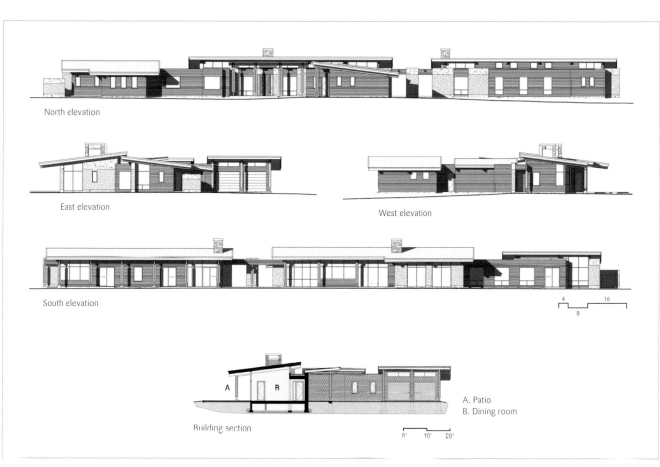

North elevation

East elevation

West elevation

South elevation

4   16
  8

Building section

A. Patio
B. Dining room

0'   10'   20'

023

The house's orientation takes advantage of passive solar gain in winter, when the sun is low. The overhang's main purpose is to block the high-angle summer sunlight.

The surrounding grain field blends into the perimeter of the house, while the glazed surfaces integrate the indoors with the outdoors.

024

Rammed-earth walls are mainly used to take advantage of their high thermal mass. This type of construction—consisting of a mix of earth and gravel. with a small amount of cement— is highly sustainable and requires little maintenance.

Interior radiant hydronic concrete floors
extend outside to become unheated
exterior concrete porches and terraces.

Energy goals were achieved via an insulation scheme that included two inches of sub-slab insulation, and used R-35 polyurethane spray foam in walls and R-63 spray foam in ceilings.

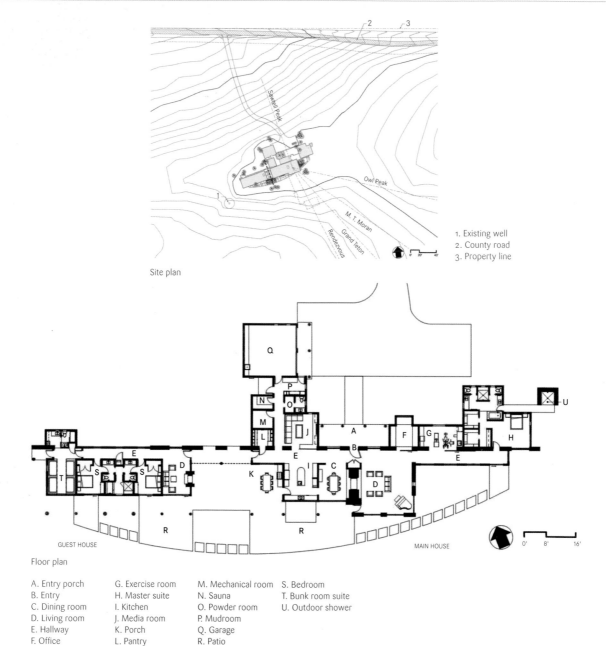

Site plan

1. Existing well
2. County road
3. Property line

Floor plan

A. Entry porch
B. Entry
C. Dining room
D. Living room
E. Hallway
F. Office
G. Exercise room
H. Master suite
I. Kitchen
J. Media room
K. Porch
L. Pantry
M. Mechanical room
N. Sauna
O. Powder room
P. Mudroom
Q. Garage
R. Patio
S. Bedroom
T. Bunk room suite
U. Outdoor shower

GUEST HOUSE

MAIN HOUSE

The entry at the north side of the house receives little natural light. But this is only to let large, open living areas facing south absorb the sun's heat energy, and take in magnificent views.

Reclaimed Douglas fir is used for soffits and sloped ceilings, while salvaged stone defines fireplaces and chimneys. Cedar siding is treated to weather naturally.

The home is heated and cooled radiantly with a high-efficiency ground source heat pump, and ventilated with a heat recovery ventilation system. Water is heated with 95 percent efficient propane on-demand water heating.

025

Environmental awareness also encourages interior designers to focus not only on the health impact of building materials, but also on their availability, cost, and the ease of installation and maintenance of materials.

026

By integrating sustainable materials into the design of buildings, it is possible to minimize the pollution and toxicity effects on the environment and on a building's occupants.

Hupomone Ranch is an original 160-acre homestead located in the Chileno Valley. The land had been fallow for more than thirty years when the owners, a young family with three children, wanted to build a barn house that would reflect their commitment to sustainable farming, and draw on the natural serenity of the site. It was also important to them to respect the character of the area, where farming and ranching are still a part of people's daily lives. The landscaping by Lutsko Associates includes several outdoor living areas, organized along a riparian restoration and native plantings. Erin Martin's interiors complement the flow of indoor-outdoor living.

Hupomone Ranch

Turnbull Griffin Haesloop Architects

Petaluma, California, United States

© David Wakely

The site has a wonderful balanced quality to it, and the simple grounded form of the barn is sited to complement this setting and capture the long views of the coastal range beyond.

027

North-facing rooms have the least natural light. To compensate for the poor natural illumination, the deep eave of the pool house slants up to take in as much light as possible, while reinforcing the visual link with the barn house.

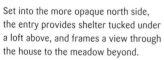

Site plan

Floor plan

Set into the more opaque north side,
the entry provides shelter tucked under
a loft above, and frames a view through
the house to the meadow beyond.

Bioclimatic diagram

The light-filled living area opens up to the long southern views and gathers the bedrooms and kitchen to either side. The kitchen has slide-away windows that open directly on the garden.

028

Windows in passive solar building are critical in spaces where there is no intention of using mechanical or electrical heating and cooling systems. Windows collect solar energy that can be used in the form of heat in the winter, and, in turn, reflect it in the summer.

029

Passive heating and cooling
with thermal mass and
insulation; geothermal, radiant
cooling and heating; and
solar and photovoltaic panels
all contribute to the house's
energy efficiency.

Green Lantern Residence

John Grable Architects

San Antonio, Texas,
United States

© Dror Baldinger,
John J. Grable Architects

Green Lantern Residence is a new one- and two-story public space addition built around an original 1948 ranch-style house. This original single-story bedroom block was kept intact, while the existing foundation and wood from a removed structure were reused for the construction of the addition. The project was developed around the architect's and client's respect for the environment. The challenge was to balance innovative sustainable technologies with time-honored techniques, while also drawing from and integrating with the historic context of the neighborhood.

030

One challenge the construction industry faces with the demolition of buildings is finding a sustainable practice for the management of waste. Identifying materials with reuse potential can reduce waste and save primary resources.

While the project incorporates systems such as photovoltaic panels, a green roof, a gray-water harvesting system, and LED lighting, there was also an effort to reduce impact through careful planning and consideration of the site and its surroundings.

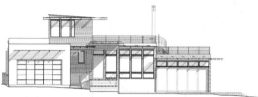

North elevation

East elevation

South elevation

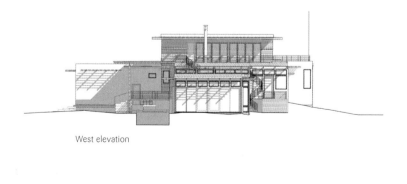

West elevation

Basement-floor plan   Ground-floor plan   Second-floor plan

1. FSC-managed wood deck
2. Fly-ash concrete
3. Natural swimming pool
4. Flexible rainwater bladders, below
5. Photovoltaic panels, above
6. Green roof

0   10'   20'   30'

032

The project was sited to
protect the heritage oak
trees found throughout the
site and to make the most of
their shade. Passive systems
such as arbors and overhang
structures were implemented
to create more shade and
reduce solar gain.

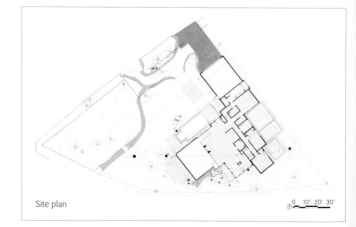

Site plan   0   10' 20' 30'

Axonometric section

Level changes affecting the public spaces provide circulation with a layer of complexity. These level changes are balanced out by an open floor plan and large windows that connect the spaces with each other, and with the outdoors.

The bridge spanning the pool creates
a strong sense of entry. This design
gesture is further enhanced by a grotto
with a waterfall that complements the
cool shade of the heritage trees residing
throughout the yard.

Wall-to-wall sliding doors in the living area open up to expand the room out into the pool and landscape, providing additional space for entertaining.

034

Split-levels open up a space, making the most of natural light and minimizing the use of artificial lighting.

035

Well-designed shading
devices, such as overhangs,
awnings and trellises, can
improve the quality of
natural lighting in an interior
space, controlling glare and
reducing contrast—ultimately,
improving visual comfort.

036

Not only is electrical lighting high energy-consuming, but it's a source of wasted heat. Energy-efficient lighting that uses both natural and electrical sources can improve lighting quality and cut cost considerably, while promoting healthier living environments.

On the second floor, a series of folding doors in a "party room" open to a large terrace in the tree canopy. The terrace steps down to its own "landscape" green roof with a hot tub that takes in distant views.

Brookline Modern Residence

ZeroEnergy Design

Brookline, Massachusetts,
United States

© Eric Roth

The Brookline Modern Residence exemplifies sophisticated modern architecture in its efficient use of space, expression through form, reserved material finishes, and a myriad of green features. In line with the homeowner's priorities, this highly insulated home features airtight construction. All the insulation is foam-free (thus avoiding the use of petroleum-based foams). On the rooftop, a solar electric system helps offset energy consumption. Cisterns capturing nearly all the storm water from the site and roof surfaces are connected to a trickle-or drip-irrigation system. Inside, consumption is limited with high-efficiency water fixtures and appliances.

WINDOWS
Windows are triple-glazed to minimize heat loss. Low-e coating on the glass maximizes the passive solar gain for improved efficiency in winter.

CENTRAL STAIRCASE
The central staircase runs from the basement to the third floor, and filters natural light from the skylight and transoms. The stack effect allows the staircase to passively pull air through the house.

LIVING B

KITCHEN B

LIVING/ KITCHEN A

BASEMENT

SLAB
A concrete slab sits on a 6-inch layer of cellular glass insulation

WALLS
Continuous exterior insulation and dense cellulose in the wall cavities achieve an R-37 value. Rigid mineral wool and cellulose were used instead of rigid foam and spray foam, being more environmentally friendly.

Sectional diagram

1. Roof insulation
2. Primary air barrier
3. Solar photovoltaic array
4. Roof deck
5. Exterior insulation (mineral wool)
6. Air barrier (self-adhered)
7. Cavity insulation (dense-packed cellulose)

The selection of modern materials complements the contemporary form. These include shiplap cedar siding, COR-TEN steel, and fiber cement panels.

Designed to accommodate multiple family generations, the paired living spaces on the first and second floors are architecturally expressed on the front façade by window systems that asymmetrically wrap around the corners of the house.

Front elevation

Right elevation

Rear elevation

Left elevation

Section 1

Section 2

A. Walk-out basement
B. Kitchen A
C. Kitchen B
D. Master bedroom 2
E. Shower room
F. Master bedroom 1
G. Study 1
H. Study 2/bedroom 3
I. Living area 2

Site plan

A. Entry
B. Bluestone patio
C. Green roof
D. Roof deck
E. Skylight
F. Photovoltaic array

Second-floor plan

Third-floor plan

A. Walk-out basement
B. Bathroom (future)
C. Laundry room
D. Mechanical room
E. Cedar closet
F. Recreational room and workshop
G. Kitchen A
H. Dining area A
I. Living area A
J. Entry
K. Study 1
L. Master bedroom 1

M. Bathroom 1
N. Patio
O. Living area B
P. Bedroom 2
Q. Bathroom 2
R. Dining area B
S. Kitchen B
T. Green Roof
U. Master bedroom 2
V. Closet/wash vanity
W. Shower
X. Roof deck

Basement-floor plan

Ground-floor plan

0'   4'   12'   48'

0'   8'   24'   48'

At the entrance, an acrylic overhang shelters foot traffic from rain. The glazed entry door opens into the family foyer, and offers visitors the possibility to proceed directly through the home to the rear outdoor living space.

037

A perfectly airtight building envelope is a critical principle of energy-efficient buildings. Any breach can lead to heat loss and unwanted air movement.

Airtight construction was achieved through continuous exterior insulation and well-insulated, triple-glazed windows.

An open stair with acrylic treads and glass rails winds from the basement to the third floor, channeling natural light down through the home.

A green roof, visible from the kitchen on the second floor, reduces rainwater runoff, while adding a natural element to the construction.

Greenlake Modern Home

Fivedot

Seattle, Washington,
United States

© Fivedot

This modern 3,300-square-foot single-family shows how sustainability is achieved through creating a symbiotic relationship between building and site. The house, which is a four-star Built Green-certified project, includes a rainwater-harvesting system that supplies the toilets and washing machine with water. On-site storm-water treatment and native and low-maintenance plants reduce its site impact. Other features include reclaimed building materials, cabinets by a local cabinet-maker, low VOC finishes, radiant floors for heating, and day-lighting strategies to reduce energy consumption.

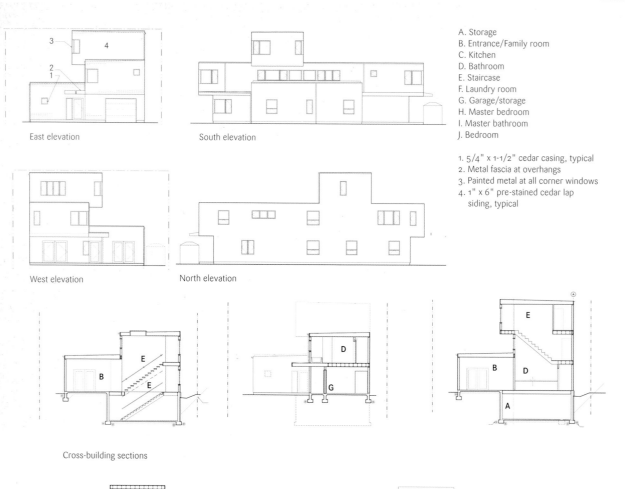

East elevation

South elevation

A. Storage
B. Entrance/Family room
C. Kitchen
D. Bathroom
E. Staircase
F. Laundry room
G. Garage/storage
H. Master bedroom
I. Master bathroom
J. Bedroom

1. 5/4" x 1-1/2" cedar casing, typical
2. Metal fascia at overhangs
3. Painted metal at all corner windows
4. 1" x 6" pre-stained cedar lap
   siding, typical

West elevation

North elevation

Cross-building sections

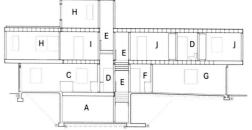

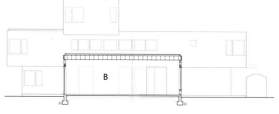

Longitudinal building sections

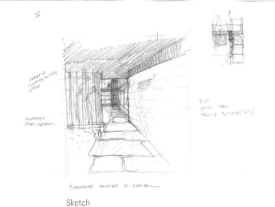

Sketch

038

The use of native plants in a landscaping project has many benefits. Native plants are often low maintenance. Once established, they can minimize soil erosion and slow down water runoff, allowing the soil to absorb the water.

The selection of materials and finishes was aimed at reducing maintenance to a minimum. The use of light colors and reflective surfaces optimizes light.

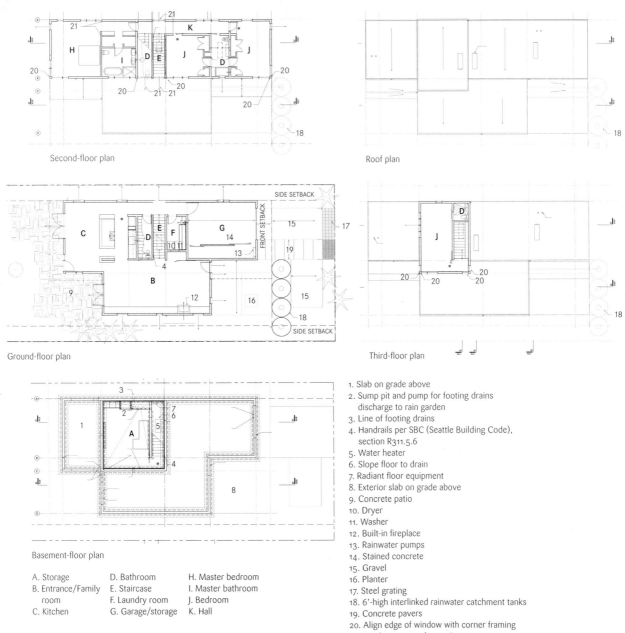

Second-floor plan

Roof plan

Ground-floor plan

SIDE SETBACK
FRONT SETBACK
SIDE SETBACK

Third-floor plan

Basement-floor plan

A. Storage
B. Entrance/Family room
C. Kitchen
D. Bathroom
E. Staircase
F. Laundry room
G. Garage/storage
H. Master bedroom
I. Master bathroom
J. Bedroom
K. Hall

1. Slab on grade above
2. Sump pit and pump for footing drains discharge to rain garden
3. Line of footing drains
4. Handrails per SBC (Seattle Building Code), section R311.5.6
5. Water heater
6. Slope floor to drain
7. Radiant floor equipment
8. Exterior slab on grade above
9. Concrete patio
10. Dryer
11. Washer
12. Built-in fireplace
13. Rainwater pumps
14. Stained concrete
15. Gravel
16. Planter
17. Steel grating
18. 6'-high interlinked rainwater catchment tanks
19. Concrete pavers
20. Align edge of window with corner framing
21. Window centered on stair

Concrete floors were used throughout the house. Their ability to retain heat makes them ideal for passive solar heating.

Situated on a large property of nearly five acres on the shores of Grand Lac Brompton, Tree House uses art as much as architecture to blend into its surroundings. Inspired by the archetypal shape of a tree, the house's first floor is covered in wood to represent a tree trunk. The much larger second floor is covered in copper tiles, representing leaves. With time, the leaves will develop a green patina, helping the house harmonize with the surrounding vegetation. With this design, the house addresses the concept of sustainability and a lifestyle in contact with nature.

Tree House

Pierre Cabana Architecte with Pierre Léveillé and Pauline Tremblay

Grand Lac Brompton, Québec, Canada

© P. Léveillé, R. Poissant

039

To realize the idea of openness to nature and integration of nature into the home, the architectural team looked for the ideal environment, construction techniques, technologies, and materials.

Northwest elevation

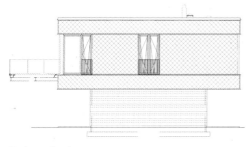

Northeast elevation

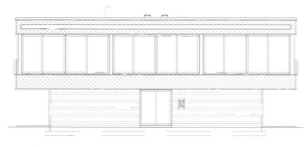

Southeast elevation

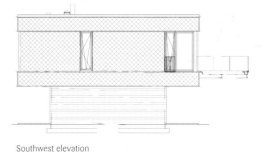

Southwest elevation

The glass wall increases the energy efficiency of the house. In winter, sunlight comes in and reduces heating costs; in summer, electric, automatic awnings keep the interior cool.

040

Insulated with great care, the house boasts excellent energy efficiency. The heating system combines geothermal energy-heated floors, a Finnish masonry heater made of soapstone, and a bi-energy—propane-electric system.

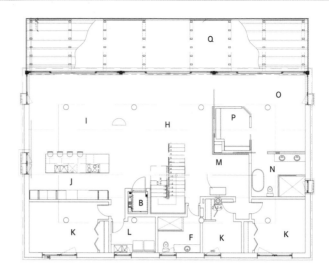

Second-floor plan

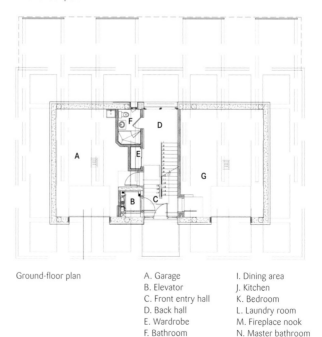

Ground-floor plan

A. Garage
B. Elevator
C. Front entry hall
D. Back hall
E. Wardrobe
F. Bathroom
G. Mechanical room
H. Living area

I. Dining area
J. Kitchen
K. Bedroom
L. Laundry room
M. Fireplace nook
N. Master bathroom
O. Master bedroom
P. Walk-in closet

A glass wall facing southeast opens onto a 760-square-foot terrace, looking out onto a panoramic view of the lake and neighboring mountains. The terrace is 180 feet above lake level, creating a sense of weightlessness and direct contact with the natural elements.

Inside, the house is friendly and warm. The combination of wood, marble, quartz, steel, glass, and porcelain creates a harmonious connection with the natural environment.

The connection with nature is especially noticeable in the spectacular, exposed beams of western fir, evoking tree branches and guiding the eye toward the lake and the surrounding forest.

In line with the exterior of the house, the interior is modern, boasting a reduced palette of contrasting finishes, such as wood and slate.

Chalet Solelyâ

Chevallier Architectes

Coupeau, Les Houches, France

© Alexandre Mermillod/
   OnixStudio

Located on a natural promontory overlooking an alpine valley and surrounded by pine forests and tall mountains, Solelyâ boasts a superb site and orientation. A preexisting house was originally self-built. Later, a new structure was added. The challenge was to avoid losing the essence of the charming and traditional original building, while integrating an updated design, modern materials and innovative construction solutions. The project was made possible by the new owners' architectural literacy, as well as their sensitivity to beauty and their appreciation for high-quality construction.

Rock faces give the house the
appearance of a natural fortress and
create a strong sense of entry. The
new structure—in aluminum and glass—
cantilevers above the massive walls,
and contrasts with the original building.

North elevation

041

In keeping with sound principles of thermal regulation, significant work went into optimizing the use of solar energy. The sun-facing façades are glazed, while those facing north have no openings.

South elevation

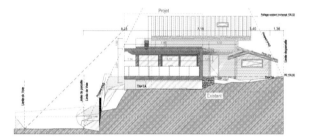

East elevation

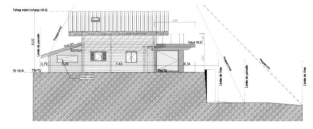

West elevation

Solelyâ is the first home with a green
roof in Coupeaux, in the commune
of Les Houches. That choice and the
work on the fifth façade resulted from
a considered process and a desire to
respect the environment.

Contrast between the old and the new structures is expressed not only through design and choice of building materials, but the way in which the different spaces function. While the original low-ceilinged structure houses private rooms, the modern addition contains common spaces designed for socializing.

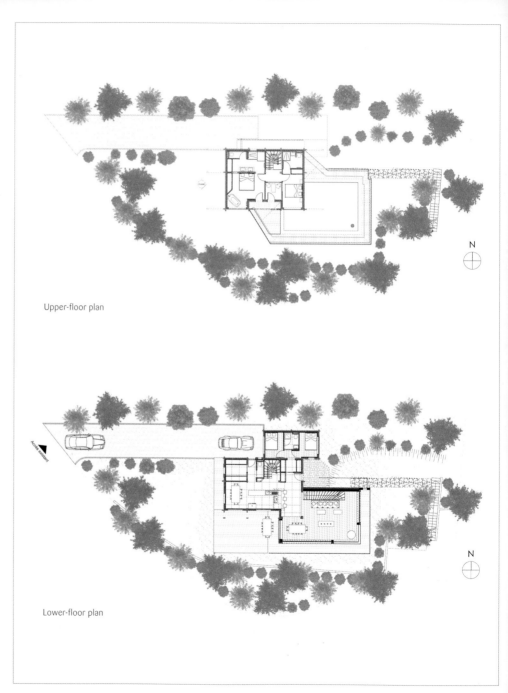

Upper-floor plan

Lower-floor plan

042

Wood is predominant in the Solelyâ chalet, in keeping with the region's traditional construction. Wood has the lowest energy consumption and lowest CO_2 emission of any commonly used building material.

043

Thermal conductivity of wood is very low compared to other materials, such as glass, stone, or steel. When it comes to acoustic properties, wood is not suitable for sound isolation, but on the other hand is ideal for sound absorption.

The main feature of the addition is a living space of generous proportions that balances out the solid construction of the original building. It satisfies the owners' desire to make the most of the exceptional site nestled into the mountains.

Room layout, on-site orientation, lighting, shading, and ventilation are key elements of passive design, which is critical to sustainable construction.

045

Used as a construction material, wood offers many environmental benefits: it is a renewable and biodegradable resource, and it is readily available. It is also easy to manipulate and transform, which makes it one of the most common building materials.

Skylights can provide a home with light and ventilation, as well as views. From an environmental standpoint, a properly installed operable skylight can be energy-efficient, minimizing lighting, cooling, and heating costs.

House in the Dunes

Stelle Lomont Rouhani Architects

Amagansett, New York,
United States

© Matthew Carbone
  Photographer

The house is situated in an environmentally sensitive area with a fragile dune-scape. The nearby ocean can be glimpsed from the second floor and roof deck. With the ocean comes the harsh salt air. The house presents a stoic façade to the street, maximizing its frontage with weather-resistant cement-board panels, which can withstand the sand and salt without aging or losing its appeal. Once inside, it becomes apparent that the backside is threading its way through the dune. The resulting volume literally hugs the dune, while providing privacy and a play of indoor and outdoor space at the same time.

Exterior materials were chosen for
their resistance to flood, wind damage,
driving rain, corrosion, and moisture.

Vertical and horizontal screens protect
the large glazed surfaces from direct
sunlight, while at the same time adding
visual interest to the house façades.

Southwest elevation

North elevation

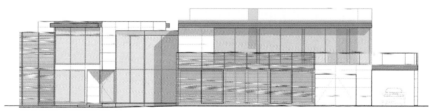

Northeast elevation

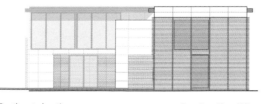

Southeast elevation

0   5   10   15 ft

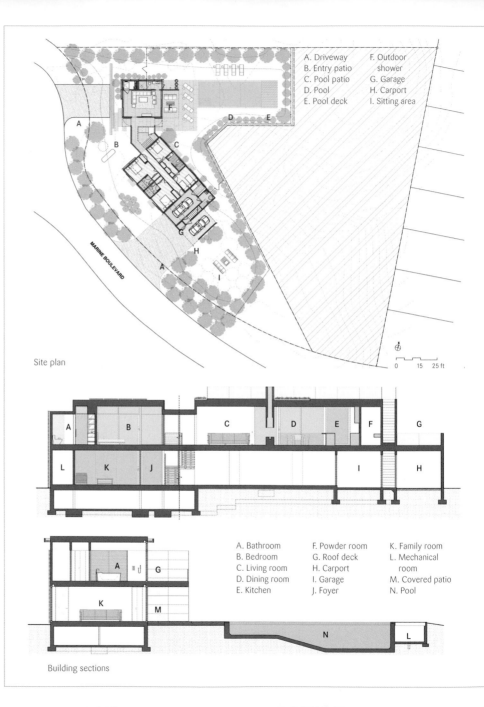

047

Solar screens are employed in both vertical and horizontal configuration to keep the energy consumption of the house down.

Site plan

A. Driveway
B. Entry patio
C. Pool patio
D. Pool
E. Pool deck
F. Outdoor shower
G. Garage
H. Carport
I. Sitting area

MARINE BOULEVARD

0   15   25 ft

Building sections

A. Bathroom
B. Bedroom
C. Living room
D. Dining room
E. Kitchen
F. Powder room
G. Roof deck
H. Carport
I. Garage
J. Foyer
K. Family room
L. Mechanical room
M. Covered patio
N. Pool

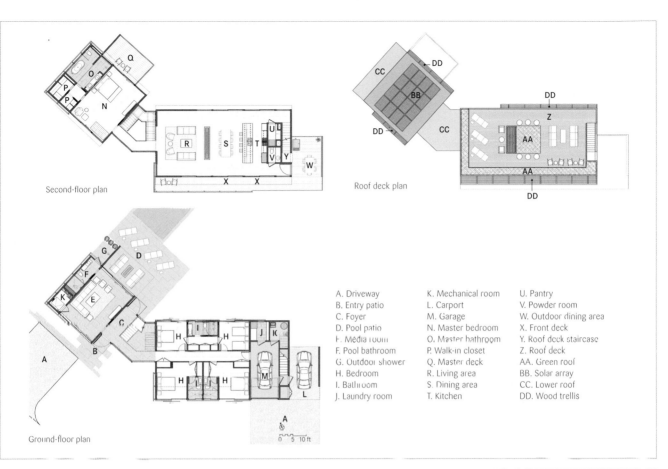

Second-floor plan

Roof deck plan

Ground-floor plan

A. Driveway
B. Entry patio
C. Foyer
D. Pool patio
E. Media room
F. Pool bathroom
G. Outdoor shower
H. Bedroom
I. Bathroom
J. Laundry room

K. Mechanical room
L. Carport
M. Garage
N. Master bedroom
O. Master bathroom
P. Walk-in closet
Q. Master deck
R. Living area
S. Dining area
T. Kitchen

U. Pantry
V. Powder room
W. Outdoor dining area
X. Front deck
Y. Roof deck staircase
Z. Roof deck
AA. Green roof
BB. Solar array
CC. Lower roof
DD. Wood trellis

0 5 10 ft

048

Atop the house is not only a habitable deck that looks out on a spectacular ocean view, but also a green roof and a place for solar panels that generate energy for the house.

Each level offers a different experience, with the lower level focusing on nestling into the dune.

The next level up reveals the expanse of the open views and offers ample opportunity to interact with the outdoors on decks.

Floor-to-ceiling windows and decks enjoying long views of the natural surroundings optimize the connection between interior and exterior.

Control/Shift House is perched on the high point of its site, taking advantage of distant views to the southeast. A gradual descending path navigates the change in terrain from the street to the entry, while a series of low retaining walls and planter beds gather and release the earth as the slope descends. The design needed to comply with the strict Homeowners Association (HOA) guidelines of the area, which included exterior massing specifications, concerning building height and length of elevations. In response to these requirements, the design process evolved from the manipulation of volumes to produce a cluster of masses of different sizes.

Control/Shift House

Matt Fajkus Architecture
Bee Cave, Texas, United States
© Charles Davis Smith

Deep overhangs provide summer shade, blocking sunlight and keeping the house cool. Based on the orientation, the overhangs project further out and slope up to allow controlled lighting into the interior.

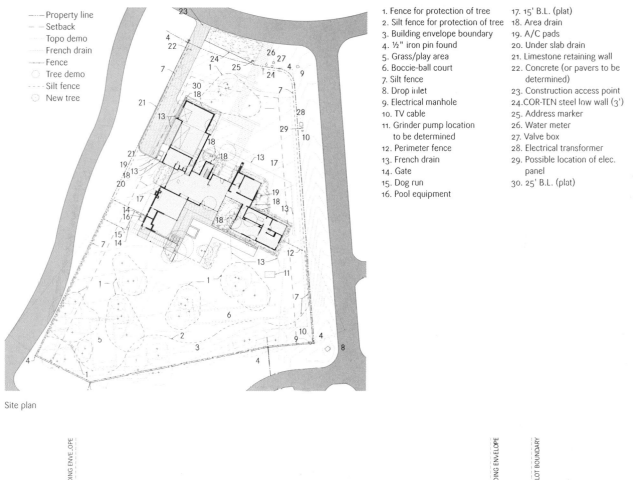

Site plan

Property line
Setback
Topo demo
French drain
Fence
○ Tree demo
Silt fence
○ New tree

1. Fence for protection of tree
2. Silt fence for protection of tree
3. Building envelope boundary
4. ½" iron pin found
5. Grass/play area
6. Boccie-ball court
7. Silt fence
8. Drop inlet
9. Electrical manhole
10. TV cable
11. Grinder pump location to be determined
12. Perimeter fence
13. French drain
14. Gate
15. Dog run
16. Pool equipment
17. 15' B.L. (plat)
18. Area drain
19. A/C pads
20. Under slab drain
21. Limestone retaining wall
22. Concrete (or pavers to be determined)
23. Construction access point
24. COR-TEN steel low wall (3')
25. Address marker
26. Water meter
27. Valve box
28. Electrical transformer
29. Possible location of elec. panel
30. 25' B.L. (plat)

Site section

LOT BOUNDARY & BUILDING ENVELOPE
BUILDING ENVELOPE
EUILDING ENVELOPE
LOT BOUNDARY
DASHED LINE INDICATES EXISTING GRADE

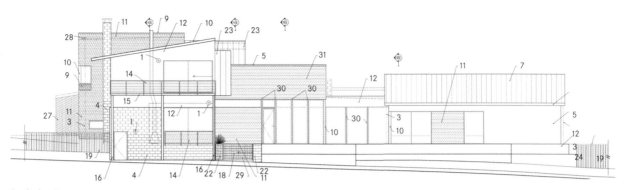

South elevation

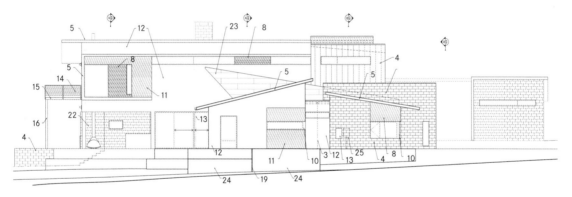

East elevation

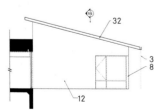

Master suite west elevation

East elevation (partial)

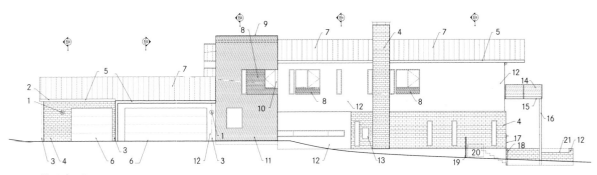

West elevation

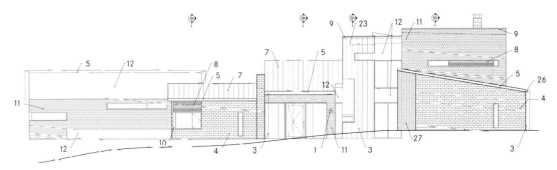

North elevation

Exterior elevation:
east stair wall

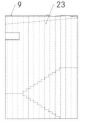

Exterior elevation:
west stair wall

1. Sconce location
2. Gutter
3. Rain chain
4. Stone
5. Paint grip sheet metal flashing
6. Paint grip sheet metal garage doors
7. Standing seam metal roof
8. Metal cladding
9. Cap flashing
10. Paint grip metal cladding
11. Horizontal tongue-and-groove siding (ipe)

12. Stucco
13. Exterior tankless water heater recessed into stone
14. Steel handrail
15. Ipe deck/painted steel frame
16. Painted steel
17. Handrail beyond
18. Rolling steel and ipe gate
19. Perimeter fence
20. Pool equipment
21. Grill
22. Stone (honed smooth)
23. Flat lock paint grip sheet metal

24. COR-TEN steel planter
25. Gas/elec. meter
26. Paint grip gutter
27. Vertical tongue-and-groove siding (ipe)
28. Through-wall scupper
29. Honed stone steps beyond
30. Tube steel
31. Horizontal tongue-and-groove soffit (ipe)
32. Paint grip sheet metal fascia

049

Voids and relief in the plan
are a natural result of this
method, and allow for light
and air to circulate throughout
every space of the house,
even into the innermost core.

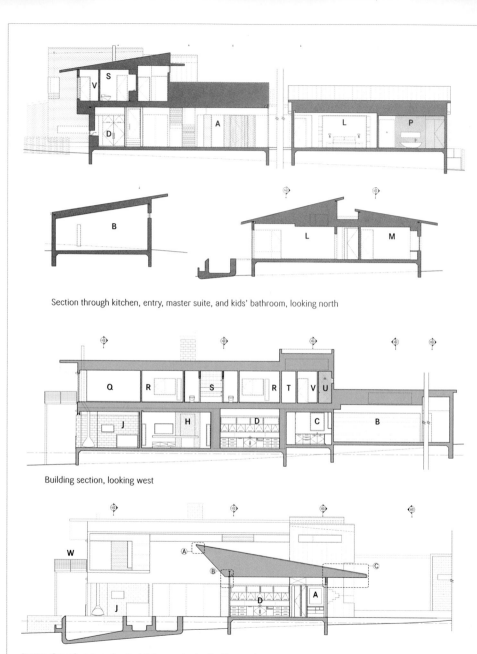

Section through kitchen, entry, master suite, and kids' bathroom, looking north

Building section, looking west

Section through screened patio, kitchen, and entry, looking west

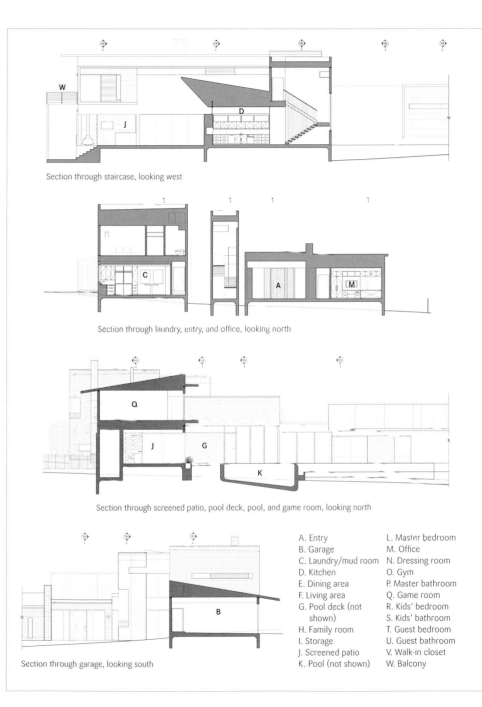

Section through staircase, looking west

Section through laundry, entry, and office, looking north

Section through screened patio, pool deck, pool, and game room, looking north

Section through garage, looking south

A. Entry
B. Garage
C. Laundry/mud room
D. Kitchen
E. Dining area
F. Living area
G. Pool deck (not shown)
H. Family room
I. Storage
J. Screened patio
K. Pool (not shown)

L. Master bedroom
M. Office
N. Dressing room
O. Gym
P. Master bathroom
Q. Game room
R. Kids' bedroom
S. Kids' bathroom
T. Guest bedroom
U. Guest bathroom
V. Walk-in closet
W. Balcony

The initial desire was for an *H*-scheme house with common entertaining spaces, bridging the gap between the more private spaces. After an investigation considering the site, program, and views, a key move was made: unfold the east wing of the *H* scheme to open all rooms to the southeast view, resulting in a *T* scheme.

The approach taken with the Control/
Shift House was to push and pull
program/massing to delineate and
define the layout of the house. Massing
is intentional, and is reiterated by
the consistent selection of materials
throughout the house.

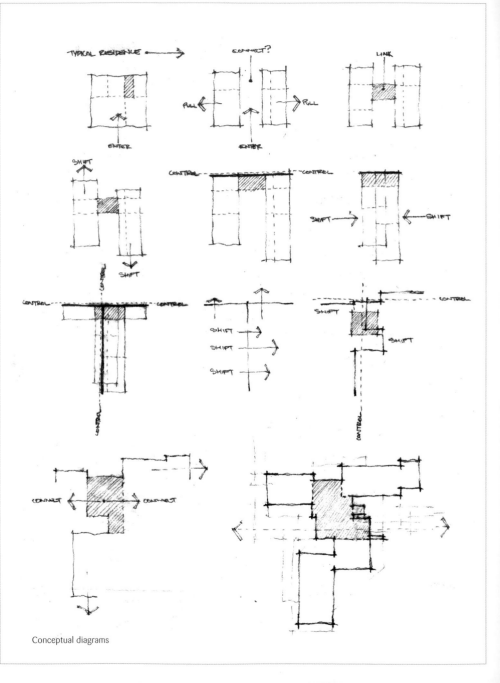

Conceptual diagrams

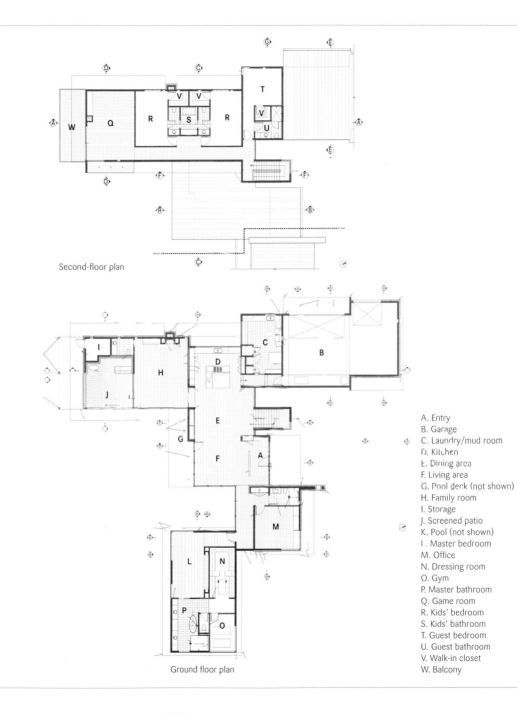

Second-floor plan

Ground floor plan

A. Entry
B. Garage
C. Laundry/mud room
D. Kitchen
E. Dining area
F. Living area
G. Pool deck (not shown)
H. Family room
I. Storage
J. Screened patio
K. Pool (not shown)
L. Master bedroom
M. Office
N. Dressing room
O. Gym
P. Master bathroom
Q. Game room
R. Kids' bedroom
S. Kids' bathroom
T. Guest bedroom
U. Guest bathroom
V. Walk-in closet
W. Balcony

The new derivation allows for both a swimming pool, which is on axis with the entry and main gathering space, and a lap pool on the cross axis extending along the lengthy edge of the master suite, and providing direct access for morning exercise and a view of the water throughout the day.

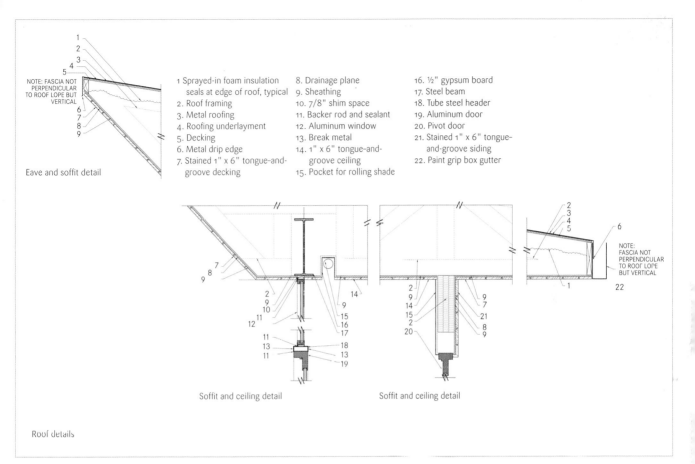

NOTE: FASCIA NOT PERPENDICULAR TO ROOF LOPE BUT VERTICAL

Eave and soffit detail

1 Sprayed-in foam insulation seals at edge of roof, typical
2. Roof framing
3. Metal roofing
4. Roofing underlayment
5. Decking
6. Metal drip edge
7. Stained 1" x 6" tongue-and-groove decking

8. Drainage plane
9. Sheathing
10. 7/8" shim space
11. Backer rod and sealant
12. Aluminum window
13. Break metal
14. 1" x 6" tongue-and-groove ceiling
15. Pocket for rolling shade

16. ½" gypsum board
17. Steel beam
18. Tube steel header
19. Aluminum door
20. Pivot door
21. Stained 1" x 6" tongue-and-groove siding
22. Paint grip box gutter

NOTE: FASCIA NOT PERPENDICULAR TO ROOF LOPE BUT VERTICAL

Soffit and ceiling detail

Soffit and ceiling detail

Roof details

The project is located in the masterplanned development of Summerlin, along the western edge of Las Vegas, at the base of Red Rock. The community's design requirements called for "design individuality, horizontality, and sensitivity to the desert hillside environment." J2 is the expression of the owners, the architects, and the developers' combined appreciation of the desert through a sensible choice of materials, environmental sensitivity, natural lighting, landscaping, and use of renewable energy sources. The building offers expanded views into an adjacent golf course and foothills in response to the client's desire to have a home that engages with its surroundings.

J2 Residence

assemblageSTUDIO

Las Vegas, Nevada,
United States

© Bill Timmerman

050

The house extends horizontally with planes of rammed earth and glass. The differing levels of transparency of the exterior walls respond to orientation in order to make the most of the views and natural light.

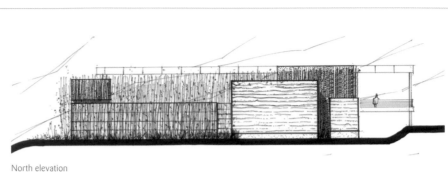

North elevation

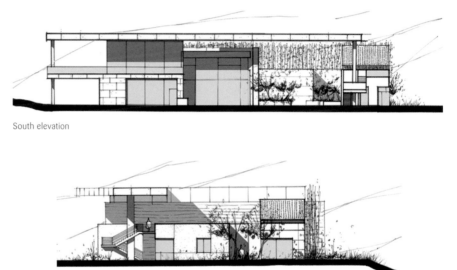

South elevation

East elevation

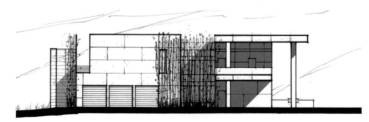

West elevation

Scale-model views

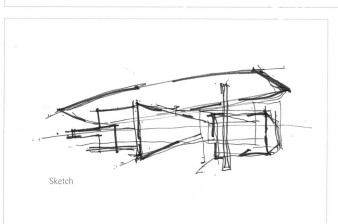

Sketch

051

A wing-shaped zinc-clad canopy was designed to prevent direct sunlight from entering the residence during the hottest season, in order to maintain acceptable levels of thermal comfort in the interior.

052

Rammed-earth construction has many environmental benefits, including temperature and noise control, pest deterrence, low maintenance, strength, and natural beauty.

053

Rammed-earth walls are extremely durable and require little maintenance other than a new sealant coat every twenty or thirty years. Because earth doesn't burn, this type of construction is ideal in fire-prone areas.

054

Interior courtyards allow for a more intimate relationship with the exterior. At the same time, the distribution of such open spaces creates spatial variety, enhancing air movement.

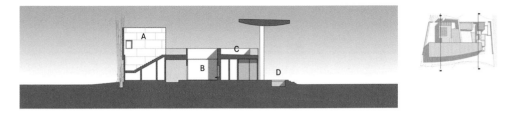

North–south sections

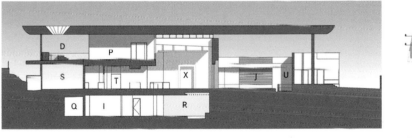

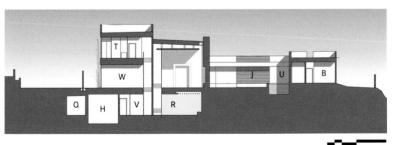

East-west sections

A. Tree house
B. Guest suite
C. Roof terrace
D. Hot tub
E. Light well
F. Exercise room
G. Electrical room
H. Home theater
I. Bar
J. Courtyard
K. Garage
L. Kitchen

M. Balcony
N. Dressing room
O. Master bathroom
P. Master bedroom
Q. Storage
R. Bowling
S. Carport
T. Kitchen
U. Pool
V. Wine cellar
W. Dining area
X. Great room

5' 10' 20'   40'

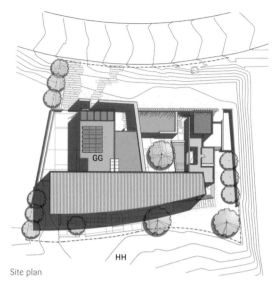

Site plan

A. Lightwell
B. Exercise room
C. Spa
D. Electrical room
E. Storage
F. Home theater
G. Wine cellar
H. Bowling
I. Bar
J. Courtyard
K. Driveway
L. Garage
M. Entry
N. Dining area
O. Great room
P. Carport
Q. Kitchen

R. Barbecue area
S. Library
T. Bedroom
U. Pool
V. Guest suite
W. Fire pit
X. Hot tub
Y. Master bedroom
Z. Balcony
AA. Master bathroom
BB. Dressing room
CC. Office
DD. Tree house
EE. Open to below
FF. Roof terrace
GG. Solar panels
HH. Golf course

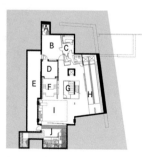

Basement-floor plan

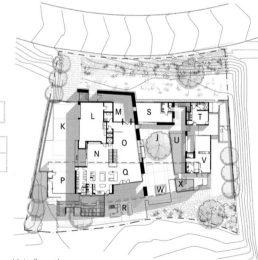

Main-floor plan

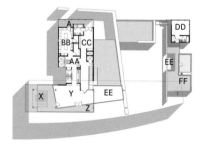

Second-floor plan

Each public space—great room, dining room, library, and guesthouse—features a view into the distant landscape, as well as intimacy with the courtyard and the pool. On the other hand, the basement bar and game room area connect with the outside through a courtyard, which admits daylight into the space.

055

A series of fins mounted underneath a skylight distributes light as it changes throughout the day. Ideally, a motorized system would follow the angle of the sun, allowing complete control over the amount and intensity of light entering an interior space.

The open plan of the house allows for a fluid interior circulation and a flexible layout. Because there are few or no obtrusions, the light from windows in exterior walls can reach deep into the core of the house.

The master bedroom has glass walls on three sides. It opens onto a balcony with a glass guardrail, allowing unobstructed views of the Red Rock Canyon.

056

A roof terrace allows visitors staying at the guesthouse to enjoy spectacular views, while being protected by the wing-canopy. The canopy accommodates Kyocera multi-crystal photovoltaic modules, which provide 40 percent of the home's power.

Desert House

Dunn & Hillam architects

Alice Springs, Northern
Territory, Australia

© Kilian O'Sullivan

Alice Springs lies within one of the most demanding
environments on Earth. Dry and extreme, the temperature
swings between highs above 113°F and lows around 21°F. When
designing the Desert House, the architectural team studied
the life of the desert closely, looking at the ways cultures have
created shade and shelter over thousands of years. As a result,
Desert House embraces the beauty and the challenge of the
desert, and manipulates the natural thermal systems to create a
living space that is immersed in the environment.

057

The house features photovoltaic panels to generate electricity, and evacuated solar tubes to transform solar energy into heat in a solar water-heating system.

Construction in harsh environments like this require the use of materials—especially for cladding—that withstand UV solar radiation.

The Desert House is a courtyard house under a fly roof, designed to put the heavily insulated interior skin of the house in the shade and to create a thermal draw of cool air from below the house, through the inner courtyard and out.

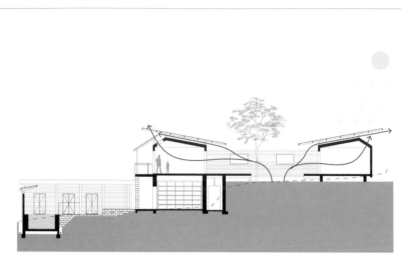

Cross-ventilation diagram

Section 1

Section 2

Second-floor plan

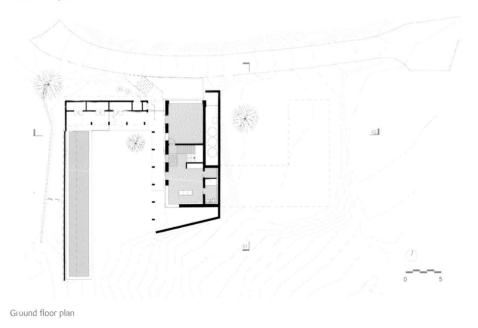

Ground floor plan

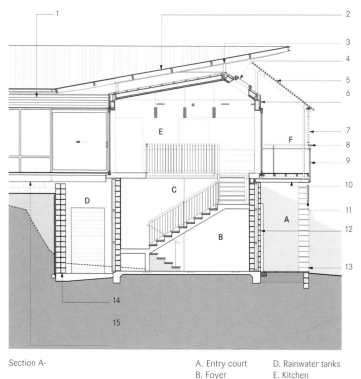

Section A-

1. 90 x 20 mm hardwood cladding screwed to 35 mm timber battens over 162 mm Structural Insulated Panels
2. Fly roof; Lysaght custom blue orb roof sheeting on framing. Underside of structure to be exposed
3. Rafters on portal upstands to main portal frame; flash through sub-roof
4. Skylight to be an electric operable skylight model VSE 2004, size S01
5. 48.2 x 2.3 mm CHS painted to match balustrade
6. Cementel Barestone cladding screwed to 35 mm battens over 162 mm Structural Insulated Panels. Internal lining to be 13 mm taped and set plasterboard with paint finish
7. Vental V80 external blinds in anodized aluminum
8. Balutrade rail to be 110 x 42 mm clear finished hardwood
9. Transit 210 stainless steel woven-mesh balustrade fixed to steel frame
10. Balcony floor; 90 x 20 mm hardwood deck on hardwood frame in removable panels over thermally independent concrete slab
11. IVR Atlas series fixed aluminum louver blades, or equivalent, in anodized finish
12. 90 mm face-block work, 50 mm air gap, sarking fixed to 90 mm framing with R1.5 mm polyester insulation, 190 mm core-filled block work. Internal lining to be 13 mm taped and set plasterboard with paint finish
13. 190 mm face block work core filled columns
14. Double 190 mm face-block work retaining wall. Retaining wall to be backed with waterproof membrane, 30 mm Elmich VersiCell, or equivalent, wrapped in geotextile fabric and installed to manufacturer's recommendations
15. Deck construction; 90 x 20 mm hardwood deck screw fixed to 200 x 42 mm hardwood joists on steel cleats to steel bearers

A. Entry court
B. Foyer
C. Staircase
D. Rainwater tanks
E. Kitchen
F. Balcony

060

The house is partly built into the hillside, taking advantage of the earth's constant temperature to minimize thermal fluctuation.

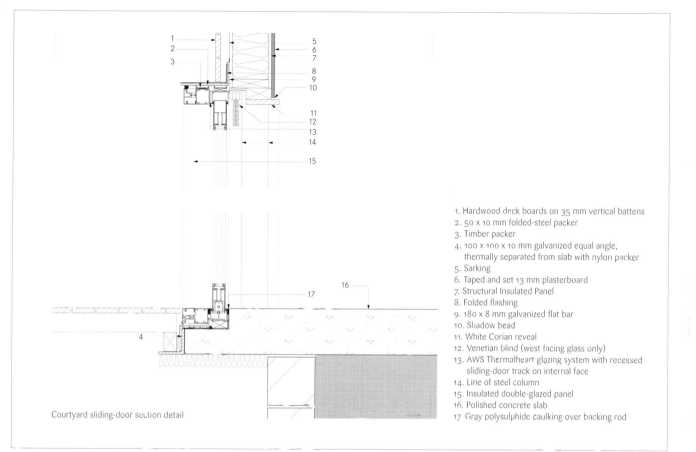

1. Hardwood deck boards on 35 mm vertical battens
2. 50 x 10 mm folded-steel packer
3. Timber packer
4. 100 x 100 x 10 mm galvanized equal angle, thermally separated from slab with nylon packer
5. Sarking
6. Taped and set 13 mm plasterboard
7. Structural Insulated Panel
8. Folded flashing
9. 180 x 8 mm galvanized flat bar
10. Shadow bead
11. White Corian reveal
12. Venetian blind (west facing glass only)
13. AWS Thermalheart glazing system with recessed sliding-door track on internal face
14. Line of steel column
15. Insulated double-glazed panel
16. Polished concrete slab
17. Gray polysulphide caulking over backing rod

Courtyard sliding-door section detail

061

When open, the sliding doors allow cool air to blow through the house and exit through operable skylights in the roof, through stack effect.

062

The courtyard is partly sheltered by deep roof eaves, protecting the glass surfaces from direct sunlight and creating a comfortable microclimate for the spaces organized around it.

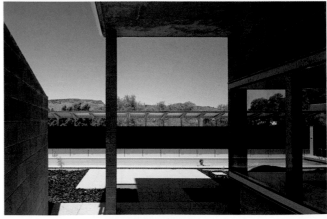

Semi-enclosed passages connect indoor spaces, offering rich spatial experiences and enhancing the relationship between the house and the natural environment.

063

Minimal mechanical systems, such as hydronically cooled and warmed slabs, are used to enhance the natural passive systems.

064

Both natural lighting and electric lighting are design elements that can enhance an architectural work. In sustainable design, electric lighting should not be used in lieu of natural lighting, but should complement it.

The building is located on the eastern hillside of El Maqui Brook, a rural section of the Chilean Coastal Range. This geographical zone is part of a protected natural reserve with high ecological value because of its singular and diverse coexisting ecosystems.

The client asked for a seasonal house surrounded by a garden, with water as the main feature. In order not to alter the rich forests and fragile ecosystems, the building was situated on a bare site. Part of the project included native plant restoration specific to the region. The east-facing siting of the house offered prolonged sunlight and optimal exposure to the prevailing ascendant air current.

Casa El Maqui

Architect: GITC

Quebrada El Maqui,
Olmué, Chile

© Felipe Díaz Contardo

A dormitory wing on the second floor projects out of the main volume to form a double-height living area. The bedrooms are oriented to the views, and exposed to the weather, while the living areas focus on their direct relationship with the garden and the water.

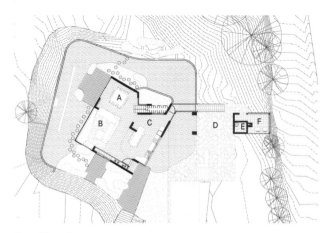

Ground-floor plan

A. Dining area
B. Living area
C. Kitchen
D. Outdoor dining
   area
E. Toilet
F. Laundry area
G. Mezzanine
H. Sitting area
I. Bathroom
J. Bedroom
K. Master bathroom
L. Master bedroom
M. Balcony

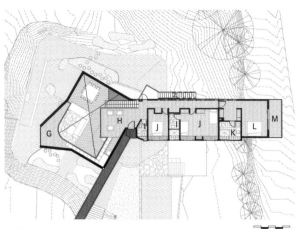

Second-floor plan

0   5 m

Section perspective   Building section

The interior layout, the volume, and the
way the building stands on and above
the ground respond to two situations,
one preexisting—the topography
and weather conditions, the other
proposed—the garden and the water.

065

The house is surrounded by a water garden, one that is not simply decorative, but is a living water filtration system. This water body also cools off the house during summer heat.

The reinforced-concrete retaining and bearing walls on the ground floor use an overlap table formwork system. They offer a solid expression and, at the same time, interact with the surroundings through its texture.

066

The steel-frame structure satisfies formal requirements and includes simple and lightweight wooden screens that allow for ventilation and the control of sunlight to maintain comfortable temperatures.

Horizon House

MF Architecture

Elgin, Texas, United States

© Bryant Hill; MF Architecture

Situated on a large lot, the house draws all movement and views toward its eastern horizon. A verdant, rolling landscape with a pond is the context for the house. Wildlife—both flora and fauna—proliferates, and Horizon House is the lens through which the elements of this environment become clear. The house is built to endure the hot climate of central Texas, from orientation to framing, and from airtightness to thermal-bridge free connections. Simple yet clever design gestures enable a free-flowing plan and section, which allow for an abundance of natural light without overheating during the hot summer days.

The composition of the house employs a simple relationship between public and private zones by directly splitting the two. This separation is reinforced by the choice of exterior cladding, with corrugated metal in the private zone and cypress siding in the public. Both speak to vernacular agricultural typologies.

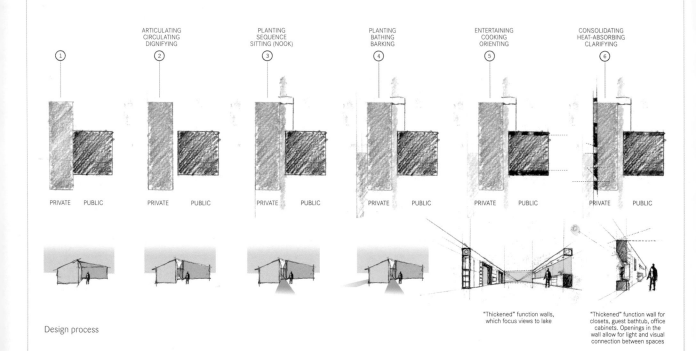

	ARTICULATING CIRCULATING DIGNIFYING	PLANTING SEQUENCE SITTING (NOOK)	PLANTING BATHING BARKING	ENTERTAINING COOKING ORIENTING	CONSOLIDATING HEAT-ABSORBING CLARIFYING
①	②	③	④	⑤	⑥

PRIVATE PUBLIC   PRIVATE PUBLIC   PRIVATE PUBLIC   PRIVATE PUBLIC   PRIVATE PUBLIC   PRIVATE PUBLIC

Design process

"Thickened" function walls, which focus views to lake

"Thickened" function wall for closets, guest bathtub, office cabinets. Openings in the wall allow for light and visual connection between spaces

The separation is further expressed through a "link." Spatially, the link is used for circulation of people, water, air, and electricity between the two sides of the home.

General notes:
· Air-conditioned space: 2,797 square feet
· Non-air-conditioned space (deck + garage): 1,662 square feet
· All existing trees to remain
· Provide underground electrical current to house
· Northwest corner of the new house to be located at a distance of 3'-1" due south from southeast corner of existing barn

1. Proposed road location
2. Private driveway
3. Possible future pool location
4. Existing cabin
5. Standing seam metal roof
6. Guest driveway
7. Existing fences
8. Existing cistern
9. Existing barn

	Existing road to remain
	Proposed new road location
	Existing road to change
	Power line
	Existing lake
	Tree cover

Site plan

067

The general contractors were required to develop a construction waste management plan vetted by a local green building certification program to recycle or reuse at least 50 percent of construction waste.

068

Energy efficiency starts by reducing heating and cooling loads through the building envelope. All windows are double-glazed, thermally broken, and employ low-e coatings.

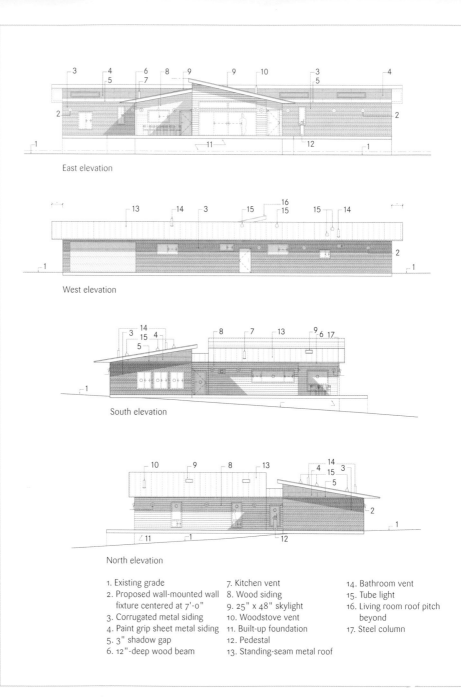

East elevation

West elevation

South elevation

North elevation

1. Existing grade
2. Proposed wall-mounted wall fixture centered at 7'-0"
3. Corrugated metal siding
4. Paint grip sheet metal siding
5. 3" shadow gap
6. 12"-deep wood beam
7. Kitchen vent
8. Wood siding
9. 25" x 48" skylight
10. Woodstove vent
11. Built-up foundation
12. Pedestal
13. Standing-seam metal roof
14. Bathroom vent
15. Tube light
16. Living room roof pitch beyond
17. Steel column

Longitudinal section 1 through kitchen and living room

069

The wall and roof employ advanced framing and insulation that exceeds local code requirements; the walls are filled with highly efficient spray-foam insulation to ensure a seamless layer.

Longitudinal section 2 through link hallway

Cross section 1 through master bedroom and kitchen

Cross section 2 through living room and guest hall

Cross section 3 through office

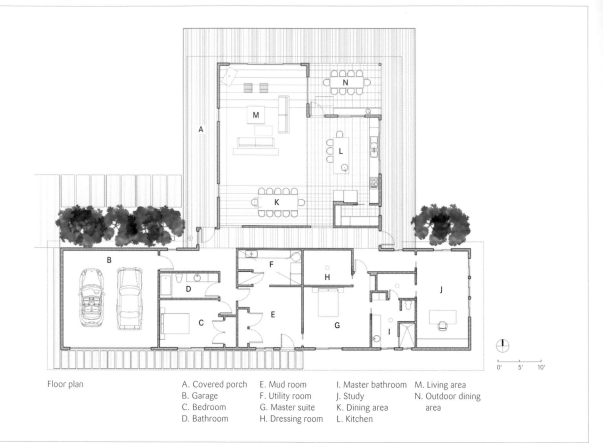

Floor plan

A. Covered porch   E. Mud room   I. Master bathroom   M. Living area
B. Garage   F. Utility room   J. Study   N. Outdoor dining
C. Bedroom   G. Master suite   K. Dining area   area
D. Bathroom   H. Dressing room   L. Kitchen

070

The design carefully integrates day lighting to reduce reliance on artificial lighting, as well as efficient cross-ventilation. High-performance equipment reduces the energy expended for conditioning the spaces and for water heating.

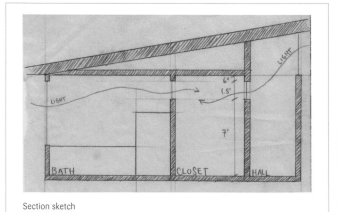

Section sketch

The outdoor and indoor connections capitalize on the dappled light from the tree and roof overhang. Various openings are carefully considered in each interior space to withstand the harsh western sun.

071

Operable windows—with double-glazing and low E coatings—provide cross ventilation, minimizing the use of a functioning air conditioning system even in the hottest months.

Elizabeth II

Bates Masi + Architects

Amagansett, New York,
United States

© Bates + Masi Architects

Too often, architecture fixates on the visual sense, with little regard for the other faculties of perception. The location of this house, in the heart of a bustling resort town, demanded special consideration of the acoustic sense. Research in architectural acoustics drove the form, materials, and detail of the house, not only shielding the property from the sound of the village, but also manipulating interior details to create a unique acoustic character for the house. This approach to the design led to a richer and more meaningful home for the family.

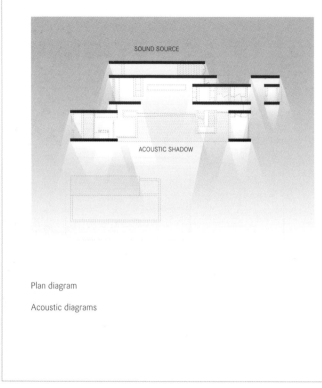

Plan diagram

Acoustic diagrams

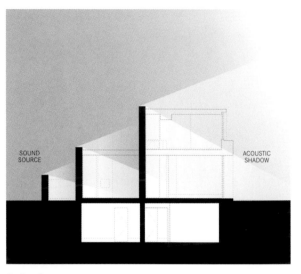

Section diagram

The house is composed of a series of parallel walls that provide layers of privacy and insulation from the noise of the nearby village. The walls project beyond the living spaces and ascend, building from a human-scale wall at the entry to a high wall along the center of the house.

072

The nearly 20-inch-thick walls have a poured concrete core wrapped in insulating foam. These walls provide excellent thermal insulation and have an extremely low sound transmission coefficient.

073

The spring-like clips hold the boards in tension against the house, while allowing for the natural movement of the wood. Traditional wood siding often fails because the natural expansion and contraction of the wood is constricted by nails.

074

The insulated walls diffract the sound waves moving past them, casting an acoustic "shadow" over the property to create a quiet outdoor gathering area.

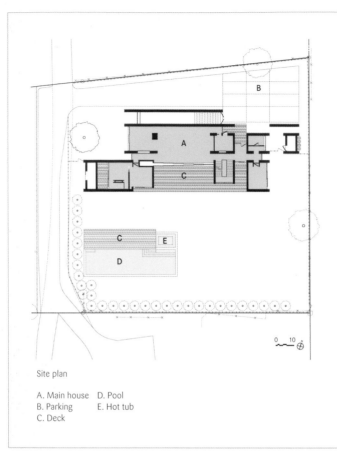

Site plan

A. Main house D. Pool
B. Parking E. Hot tub
C. Deck

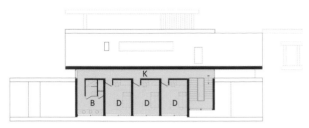

Second-floor plan

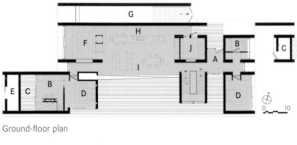

Ground-floor plan

A. Entry vestibule G. Open to below
B. Bathroom H. Kitchen
C. Outdoor shower I. Living/dining area
D. Bedroom J. Laundry room
E. Storage K. Hallway
F. Family room

Due to the strength of their concrete
cores, the walls act as structural beams,
enabling them to run the full length of
the gathering space at the center of the
house and the covered deck.

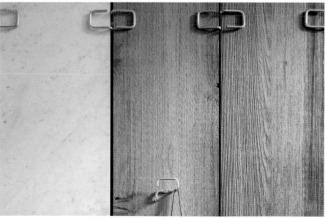

075

Inside, variations on the clips are used as robe hooks, cabinet pulls, and hinges for an adjustable sound baffle in the central gathering space.

076

Sound waves passing through the gaps between the cedar boards and absorbed by a felt panel. The hinges allow the spacing of the boards to be adjusted so the room can be acoustically tuned for intimate gatherings or boisterous parties.

The staircase is also tuned to create
a subtle acoustic experience. The
treads taper in thickness, changing
the pitch of footfalls as one ascends
from the woodshop in the basement,
past the main floor with public spaces,
guest room, and master bedroom, the
children's rooms on the upper floor.

Bluebell Pool House

Adam Knibb Architects

Winchester, Hampshire,
United Kingdom
© Ben Savage

The clients' brief called for the creation of a pool house to replace a disused tennis court. Their desire for a self-build project required a design that would allow for simplified building processes facilitated by a prefabricated timber structure.

The new construction harnesses nature, maximizes views, and minimizes environmental impact. Sited with its "back" to woodland, the pool house is a folded rectangular form that frames views across the garden and fields. The design links movement from public to private areas through purposively designed elements, which promote fluidity rather than physical separation. The decking acts as a "catwalk," enhancing the experience.

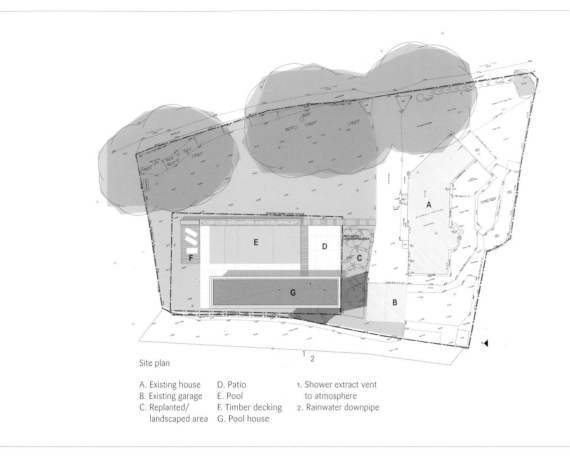

Site plan

A. Existing house
B. Existing garage
C. Replanted/
   landscaped area
D. Patio
E. Pool
F. Timber decking
G. Pool house

1. Shower extract vent
   to atmosphere
2. Rainwater downpipe

Designed to respond to its surroundings, the pool house is clad in timber, with a vertical orientation to mimic the trees. Natural oak cladding, softening over time, and a sedum roof help the building blend further into the environment.

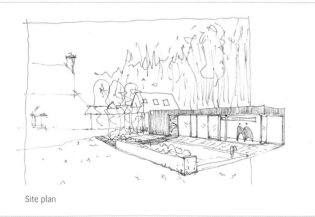

Site plan

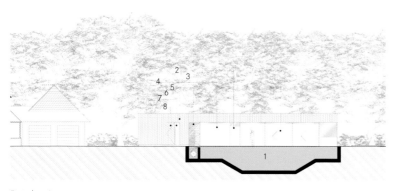

East elevation

South elevation

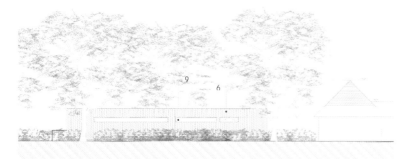

West elevation

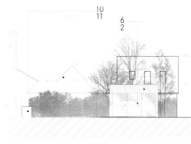

South elevation

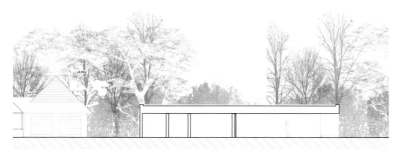

East section

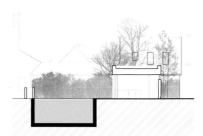

North section

1. Pool
2. Double glass sliding doors
3. Aluminum solid panel, mid gray
4. Fixed window
5. Stable door, oak clad
6. Vertical oak cladding
7. Opaque glass
8. Shower room door
9. High level slot windows
10. Planter
11. Existing house in background

077

A sedum roof not only contributes to temperature control, but helps to minimize visual impact of a built structure and building maintenance. High levels of insulation combine with a sedum roof to minimize a building's internal heat fluctuations.

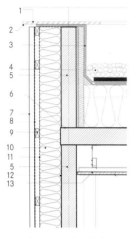

Parapet section detail

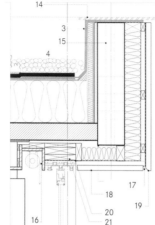

Parapet and glazing head detail

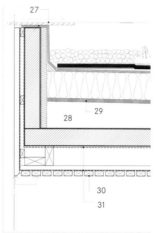

Parapet section detail

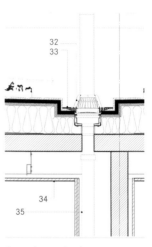

Flat roof-gutter detail

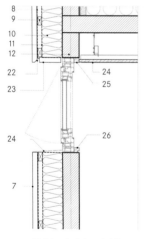

High-level window detail

1. 5 mm steel sheet as coping fixed through to parapet. MIO painted
2. 8 mm water-drip notch
3. Flat roof waterproofing barrier lapped up and underneath coping
4. Gravel border
5. 94 mm CLT wall panel
6. CTL structure
7. 50 x 22 mm vertical oak cladding
8. Black insect mesh
9. 25 mm air gap with diagonal battens fixed through CLT structure
10. 125 mm Kingspan K12 rigid insulation
11. Continuous vapor membrane
12. Steel post
13. MF suspended ceiling with 12.5 mm plasterboard, skimmed and painted

14. 15 mm steel sheet as coping, fixed through parapet. MIO painted
15. Glulam beam
16. Recessed blind box
17. 10 mm ventilation gap with insect mesh
18. 50 x 22 mm oak cladding, laid on soffit, to follow lines from façade
19. Vertical cladding to have 45-degree chamfer on exposed edge
20. Vapor barrier to continue behind glazing track
21. SW timber packing as required
22. 45-degree chamfer for water drip. Continuous insect mesh
23. 30 mm oak plank to window head reveal

24. PPC aluminum window sill. Part of window package. To be installed post cladding
25. 30 mm MDF window reveal lining
26. 30 mm MDF window reveal lining with 100 mm shadow gap to wall
27. Coping to have slight fall into fall roof
28. Timber furring to create fall of 1:60
29. 18 mm WBP plywood deck
30. Oak battens to clad soffit
31. Insect mesh and vapor barrier
32. Leaf guard to all outlets
33. 300 mm wide gutter trough
34. 12.5 mm plasterboard, skimmed and painted on MF suspended ceiling
35. Internal RWP

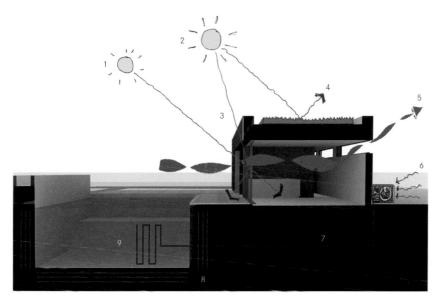

Environmental strategy diagram

1. Winter sun
2. Summer sun
3. Recessed glazing to minimize summer solar gains
4. Sedum roof. Provides habitat and reflects heat
5. Natural ventilation flows through building
6. Air-source heat pump intake
7. Air-source heat pump supplying pool heat
8. Sunken swimming pool to increase thermal mass, reducing heat loss
9. Air-source heat pump supplying subfloor heating

078

An air-source heat pump not only provides renewable energy to heat both the pool and subfloor heating system, but also significantly reduces running costs. An extremely efficient pool cover was also chosen to minimize heat loss.

079

The prefabricated approach reduced construction time dramatically. The sustainable oak cladding was sourced from English woodlands and sized for minimum wastage.

Large sliding doors blur the boundaries between interior and exterior spaces. Large glazed surfaces help maximize solar gain during winter months. Set back under a parapet overhang, they contribute to temperature control during summer months.

080

The Pool House was designed to be sustainable in construction and use. The timber structure allowed use of a renewable source, reduced CO_2 emissions, and aided carbon storing within the building.

081

Wood siding is a fast-growing trend that can contribute to a building's sustainable footprint. Oak wood is durable and perfectly suitable for exterior use. It is available with FSC certification.

House E

Caramel Architekten
Linz, Austria
© Martin Pröll

The two-story House E sits on a plot of land offering spectacular views of Linz, with the main floor at about 20 feet above street level to take full advantage of these views. Despite the pronounced slope of the site, the configuration of the house allows for a garden area to adjoin the living area on the same level to the west and north, even with the extreme slope. Since regulations permitted construction only up to 2,150 square feet per story, it was not easy to accommodate a spatial plan for a family of five, especially since all the primary functions were to be arranged in a single floor.

082

Never underestimate the importance of a driveway. When well designed, it makes for a strong sense of arrival. In this case, House E's garage is partially excavated from the hillside, minimizing its visual impact.

Site plan

The cantilevered roof covers wide-ranging terraces that feature wooden flooring that continues from the spacious halls in the living areas, and protects the interiors from direct sunlight. The inner and outer living areas are separated solely by large glazed surfaces, sections of which are openable.

083

Building on a slope often requires a high level of design consideration. The design must suit the incline of the terrain, solar orientation, site access, and a functional layout.

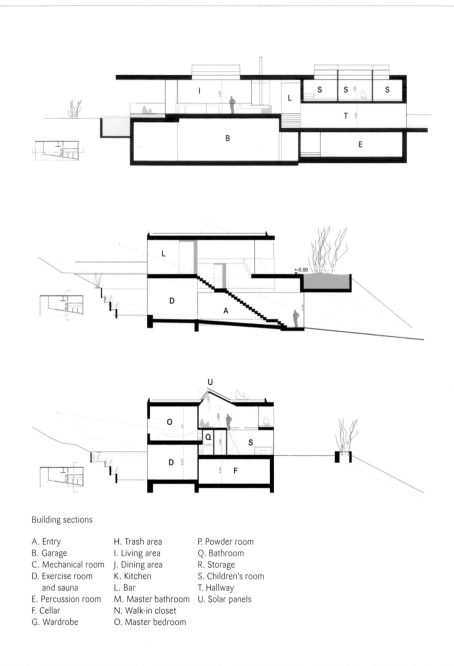

Building sections

A. Entry
B. Garage
C. Mechanical room
D. Exercise room
   and sauna
E. Percussion room
F. Cellar
G. Wardrobe

H. Trash area
I. Living area
J. Dining area
K. Kitchen
L. Bar
M. Master bathroom
N. Walk-in closet
O. Master bedroom

P. Powder room
Q. Bathroom
R. Storage
S. Children's room
T. Hallway
U. Solar panels

084

The house is low and horizontal, with most rooms arranged on a split-level above the garage floor. Staggered levels are connected by flights of stairs, promoting an open-plan layout, while separating areas of different functions.

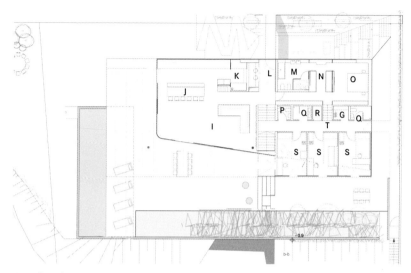

Upper-floor plan

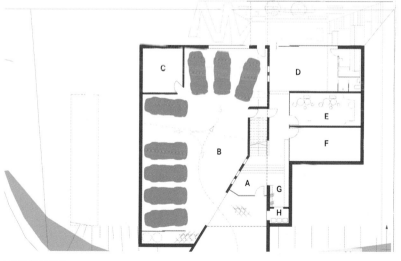

Lower-floor plan

085

Excavation and retaining wall construction costs can be minimized when designing a home that adapts well to the unique slope of a terrain.

Minimally framed floor-to-ceiling windows enhance the open character of the living area, while minimizing the visual boundaries between the interior and the exterior.

The sauna, on the lower floor, opens
up onto a discreet rock garden on the
northern side of the house.

The W.I.N.D. House

UnsStudio

North Holland, The Netherlands

© Fedde de Weert,
Inga Powilleit

Just as comprehensive sustainability is not merely about providing designs with visibly "green" features, so is home automation technology not about displaying futuristic devices like designers did in the predictive show homes of the last century.

The W.I.N.D. House is an example of how contemporary smart homes respond to changes in today's lifestyles by enabling the control of appliances from afar and by incorporating the necessary installations to aim for a zero-net-energy building. Flexible floor plans allow for diversity in function (gathering, seclusion, work, play) according to a family's changing needs.

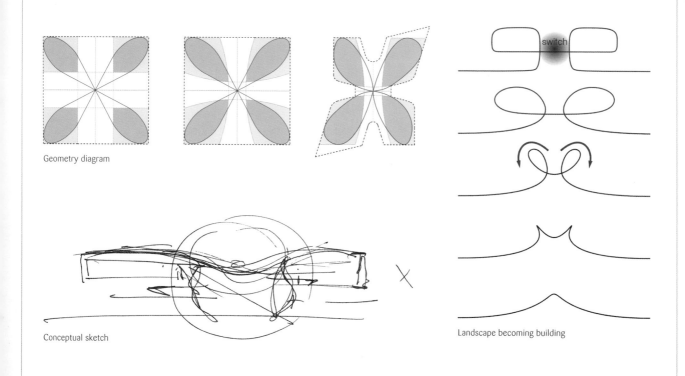

Geometry diagram

Conceptual sketch

switch

Landscape becoming building

Suggesting the shape of a simple flower, each of the four façades curves toward the center to create four distinct petal-like wings.

The lobular design of the house draws the landscape deeper into the interior and strengthens the visual connection between the different wings through their glazed façades.

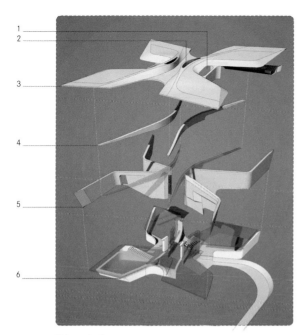

1. Skylight
2. Light shafts
3. Roof leaves
4. Pair cantilevering beams
5. Structural wings
6. Programmatic plinth

Volumetric diagram 1

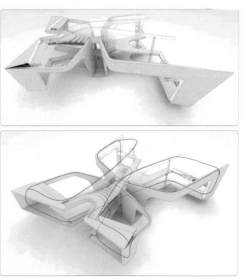

Volumetric diagram 2

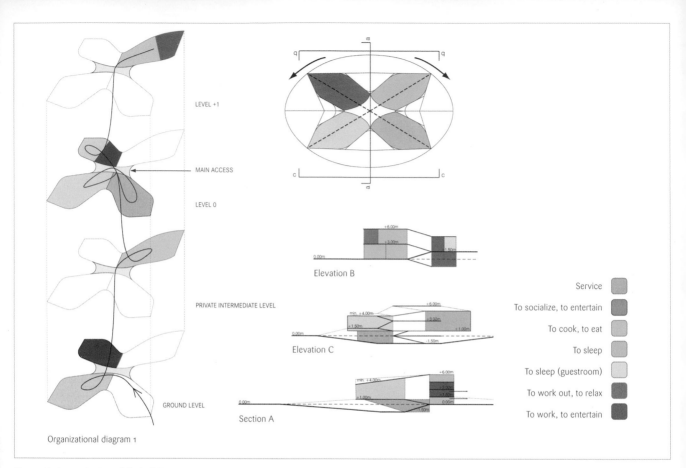

LEVEL +1

MAIN ACCESS

LEVEL 0

PRIVATE INTERMEDIATE LEVEL

GROUND LEVEL

Organizational diagram 1

Elevation B

Elevation C

Section A

Service

To socialize, to entertain

To cook, to eat

To sleep

To sleep (guestroom)

To work out, to relax

To work, to entertain

The vertical organization of the building follows a centrifugal split-level principle. An open staircase at the center of the house connects the front and back wings, while providing expansive vistas through the house and out toward the surrounding landscape.

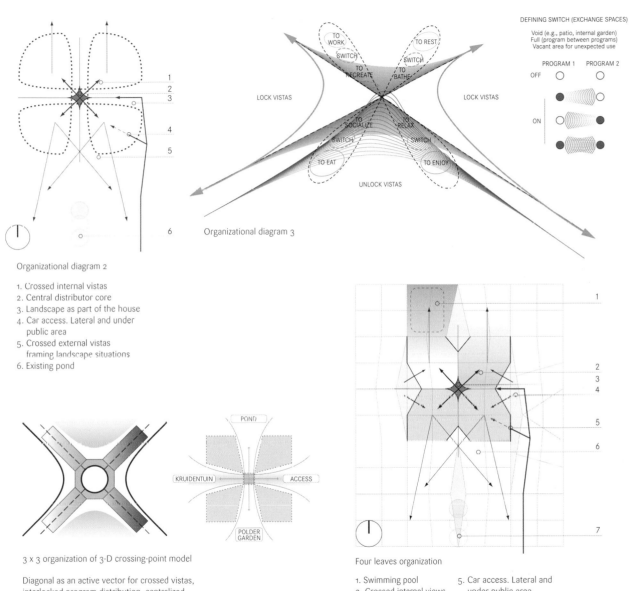

Organizational diagram 3

DEFINING SWITCH (EXCHANGE SPACES)

Void (e.g., patio, internal garden)
Full (program between programs)
Vacant area for unexpected use

LOCK VISTAS

UNLOCK VISTAS

TO WORK
TO REST
SWITCH
SWITCH
TO RECREATE
TO BATHE
TO SOCIALIZE
TO RELAX
SWITCH
SWITCH
TO EAT
TO ENJOY

Organizational diagram 2

1. Crossed internal vistas
2. Central distributor core
3. Landscape as part of the house
4. Car access. Lateral and under public area
5. Crossed external vistas framing landscape situations
6. Existing pond

3 x 3 organization of 3-D crossing-point model

Diagonal as an active vector for crossed vistas, interlocked program distribution, centralized infrastructure, voids and landscape integrated into everyday life.

POND

KRUIDENTUIN   ACCESS

POLDER GARDEN

Four leaves organization

1. Swimming pool
2. Crossed internal views
3. Central distributor core
4. Landscape as part of the house
5. Car access. Lateral and under public area
6. Crossed external vistas framing landscape situations
7. Existing pond

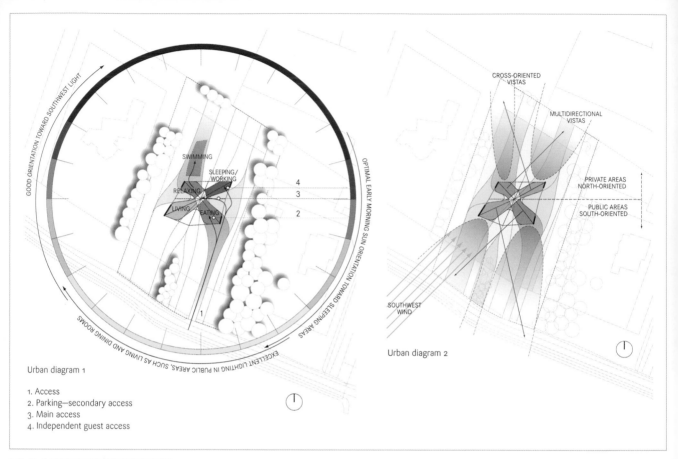

GOOD ORIENTATION TOWARD SOUTHWEST LIGHT

OPTIMAL EARLY MORNING SUN ORIENTATION TOWARD SLEEPING AREAS

EXCELLENT LIGHTING IN PUBLIC AREAS, SUCH AS LIVING AND DINING ROOMS

SWIMMING

SLEEPING/
WORKING

RELAXING

LIVING   EATING

4

3

2

1

Urban diagram 1

1. Access
2. Parking—secondary access
3. Main access
4. Independent guest access

CROSS-ORIENTED
VISTAS

MULTIDIRECTIONAL
VISTAS

PRIVATE AREAS
NORTH-ORIENTED

PUBLIC AREAS
SOUTH-ORIENTED

SOUTHWEST
WIND

Urban diagram 2

086

The segmentation of the house allows for a clear separation of functions. This configuration, devoid of corridors, allows for a more effective use of space, and a more efficient use of energy.

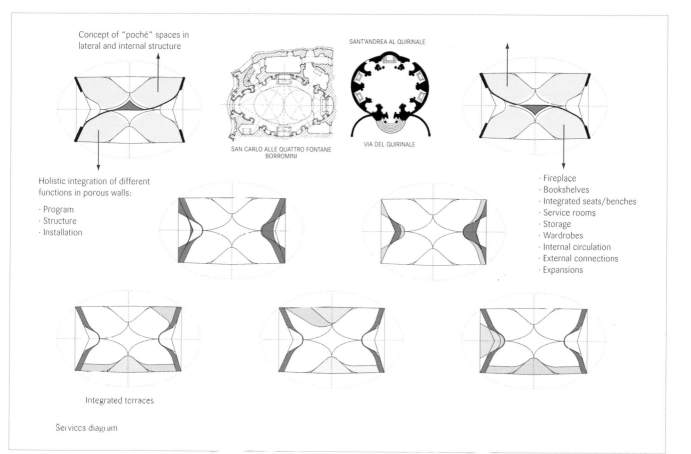

Concept of "poché" spaces in lateral and internal structure

SANT'ANDREA AL QUIRINALE

SAN CARLO ALLE QUATTRO FONTANE
BORROMINI

VIA DEL QUIRINALE

Holistic integration of different
functions in porous walls:

· Program
· Structure
· Installation

· Fireplace
· Bookshelves
· Integrated seats/benches
· Service rooms
· Storage
· Wardrobes
· Internal circulation
· External connections
· Expansions

Integrated terraces

Services diagram

087

Service rooms, storage, and bookshelves can double as interior partitions, optimizing space, and creating a more porous environment.

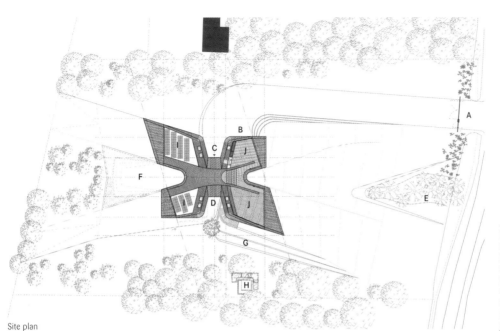

Site plan

A. Entrance gate
B. Carport
C. Main entrance
D. Entrance garden
E. Pond
F. Swimming pond
G. Herb garden
H. Condenser heat pump
I. Solar panels
J. Roof terrace

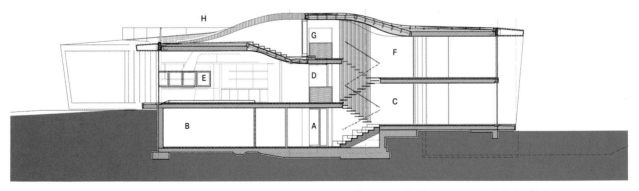

Building section

A. Hall at entrance level
B. Basement/storage
C. Gallery at playroom/music room level
D. Hall at living/dining level
E. Kitchen/dining
F. Gallery at master bedroom level
G. Hall at access to roof terrace level
H. Roof terrace

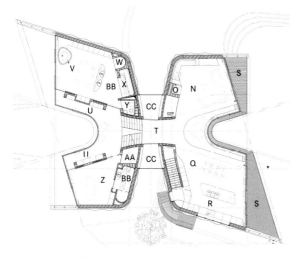

Second-floor plan

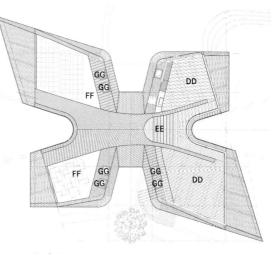

Roof plan

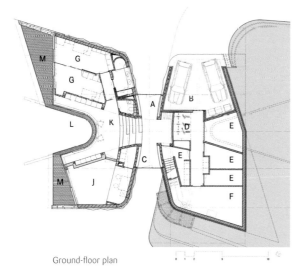

Ground-floor plan

A. Main entrance
B. Carport
C. Entrance garden
D. Bicycle storage
E. Storage
F. Technical equipment
G. Children's rooms
H. Bathroom
I. Toilet
J. Music Room
K. Gallery
L. Swimming pond
M. Terrace

N. Living room
O. Fireplace
P. Podium
Q. Dining
R. Kitchen
S. Terrace
T. Hall
U. Gallery
V. Master bedroom
W. Shower
X. Turkish bath
Y. Toilet
Z. Guest room

AA. Storage
BB. Bathroom
CC. Void
DD. Roof terrace
EE. Stair to roof Terrace
FF. Solar panels
GG. Roof window

088

Exterior canopies and side walls strengthen the indoor-outdoor connection by framing the view toward the landscape and providing sheltered outdoor spaces. These side walls are predominantly solid, providing privacy from the neighboring buildings.

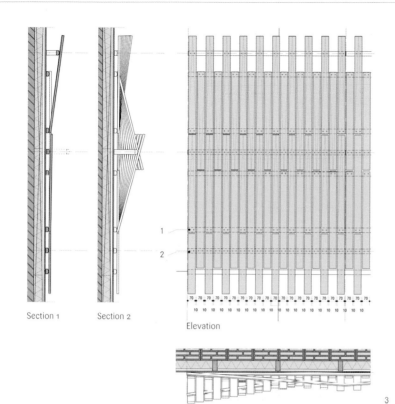

Section 1   Section 2

Elevation

1
2

Plan view

3

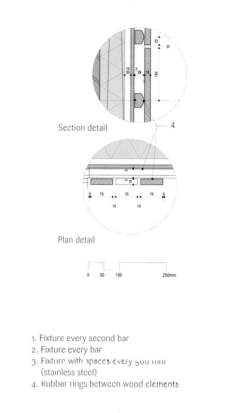

Section detail   4

Plan detail

0   50   100   250mm

1. Fixture every second bar
2. Fixture every bar
3. Fixture with spaces every 500 mm
   (stainless steel)
4. Rubber rings between wood elements

The façade and the roof are clad with wooden slats that, in specific areas, taper in and out, providing a play of light and shadow, while also acting as screens for the windows in the kitchen and bathroom behind.

The wooden slat detail is carried out to the eaves of the house, providing the glazed surfaces with shade. At the same time, they provide the wooden shell of the building with various degrees of transparency, responding to privacy and shading needs.

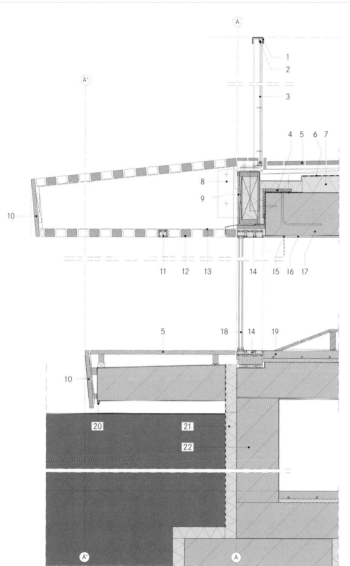

1. Balustrade: steel U-profile 80 x 45 mm (WxH)
2. Tension cable stainless steel
3. Nylon net
4. Steel plate 200 x 200 x 2 mm
5. Wood terrace deck
6. Watertight layer
7. Sloped walkable insulation layer
8. Steel plate, 15 mm (for canopy every 900 mm, for balustrade every 1,800 mm)
9. Cement panel
10. Laminated wood panel, uncoated and naturally preserved
11. Integrated lighting fixtures
12. Wood bars
13. Rubber strips
14. Aluminum sliding frames
15. Integrated curtain rail
16. Wide-slab concrete floor
17. Evaporating clay stucco layer
18. HR++ double glazing
19. Screen with floor heating and cooling
20. Integrated hidden LED-lighting fixture
21. Shockproof, water-resistant insulation
22. Concrete wall

Vertical detail section

089

The roof is divided into two areas, one accessible, the other equipped with solar panels. The sustainability concept of the house boasts an air/water heat pump for heating and cooling, and mechanical ventilation with waste-heat recovery.

The comprehensive assimilation of the surrounding landscape and a centrifugal circulation form the basis of the design. This strategy is aimed at creating an interior with various degrees of porosity, responding to the different levels of privacy required by the occupants of the house.

The spatial configuration of wings/
rooms is in response to the varying
degrees of flexibility, sustainability, and
interaction required by the owners.

090

Heat gain is reduced through the use of tinted glass on the fully glazed front and back façades. This coated glazing enables natural light to flood interior spaces, while maintaining privacy during daytime.

The W.I.N.D. House is backed by a
sheltered wooded area and fronted
by a large, open expanse of polder
landscape. The design of the house
responds both to its setting and to the
seasons, mitigating or enhancing their
effects, as needed.

Almost all floors are homogeneously covered with a polyurethane coating in soft tones to increase the fluid connection among all areas. The sleeping areas have a slightly darker tone to emphasize the intimacy of these spaces.

The more enclosed rooms –including sauna and bathrooms—are located around the core of the house, responding to privacy requirements. Still, they benefit from natural light through skylights to compensate for the lack of windows.

Fenwick Street House

Julie Firkin Architects

Clifton Hill, Victoria, Australia
© Christine Francis

This design was developed to maximize the available light and space on an oddly shaped block. The original weatherboard cottage, which addresses the street, has been retained while a two-level addition at the rear provides a new kitchen and dining areas, as well as a master bedroom suite. The character of the natural materials such as timber and concrete is expressed against white surfaces with occasional moments of strong color.

Silvertop ash clads both the addition's
exterior and interior, alluding to
the original weatherboard cottage,
while giving the new structure a
contemporary look.

The addition is angular and tapered in form, with an overhanging upper level, which permits the living spaces to be drenched in light in winter, and enjoy shade in summer.

East elevation

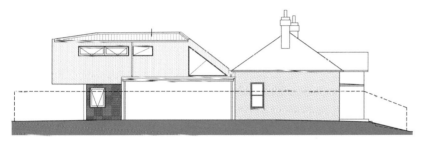

South elevation

North elevation

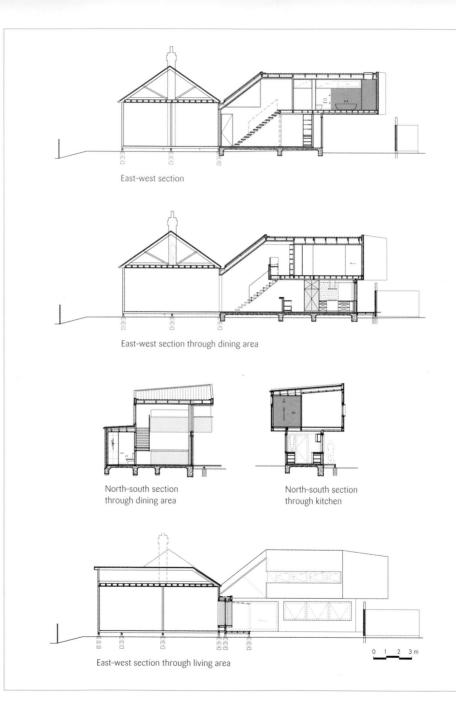

091

Helping to facilitate passive solar heating and cooling, the roof connects the existing cottage with the new extension. It allows abundant natural light to drench the double-height space through large clerestory windows.

East–west section

East–west section through dining area

North–south section
through dining area

North–south section
through kitchen

East–west section through living area

0 1 2 3m

Inside, a variety of subtly overlapping spatial volumes is achieved within a relatively simple overall form. Interior finishes are light-colored so as to be reflective.

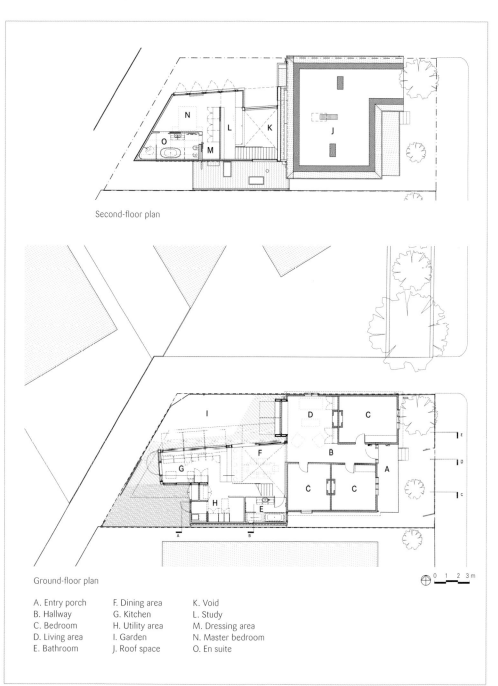

Second-floor plan

Ground-floor plan

A. Entry porch
B. Hallway
C. Bedroom
D. Living area
E. Bathroom
F. Dining area
G. Kitchen
H. Utility area
I. Garden
J. Roof space
K. Void
L. Study
M. Dressing area
N. Master bedroom
O. En suite

0 1 2 3 m

The wood-clad addition clearly stands out from the original white weatherboard cottage, both in its form and finish. At the same time, it provides ample social spaces strongly connected with the outdoors.

092

Windows are critical elements in passive solar homes. The design for this house typology responds to the specifics of a region's climate, but window guidelines are universal. They are oriented and sized to maximize heat gain in winter and minimize it in summer.

The dining area, adjacent to the open kitchen, is the double-height link between the existing home and the extension. It boasts large sliding-glass doors that open the interior to the wood deck outside.

093

The study on the second floor receives natural lighting from the north slantwise. North-facing windows produce even light, little glare, and virtually no unwanted summer heat gain.

A transom window above the soaking tub and a skylight above the shower provide the bathroom with the necessary privacy without sacrificing natural lighting.

SlrSrf

Open Source Architecture

Culver City, California,
United States

© Benny Chan/Photoworks

SlrSrf is a compact project that embeds performance
characteristics into an architectural surface. Optimization of
the roof as a solar-receiving surface for net-zero photovoltaic
electrical production generates the form of a 450-square-foot
addition and the renovation of an existing house. The project
responds to programmatic requirements, while incorporating
sustainable design solutions. The architectural design is linked
to current technological advances, which, according to the
designers' philosophy, are connected to contemporary culture
and environmental conditions, which promote investigation
of innovative design processes and experimentation with new
materials.

094

The rotation of the roof surface maximizes solar intensity for the photovoltaic panels. This creates an opportunity for thickening the north wall, inside which heating and cooling systems can be placed.

Existing conditions

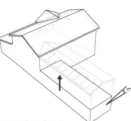

Optimal roof angle for photovoltaic panel: 17 degrees

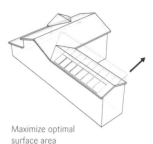

Maximize optimal surface area

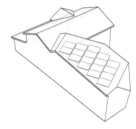

Rotate roof and photovoltaic panels to optimal orientation (south)

Shift panels to reduce overhang

Final optimized roof

Temperature distribution diagram

Temperature distribution diagram for second floor, east wing

Ground-floor plan

Second-floor plan

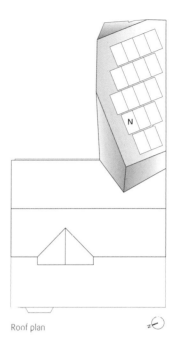

Roof plan

A. Existing living room
B. Existing bedroom
C. Study
D. Library
E. Bedroom

F. Kitchen
G. Bathroom
H. Master bathroom
I. Storage
J. Master bedroom

K. Children's bathroom
L. Children's playroom
M. Bridge
N. Photovoltaic panels

A. Existing house
B. Existing garage
C. Driveway
D. Landscaping
E. 5'-foot tall
  CMU wall

Aerial view

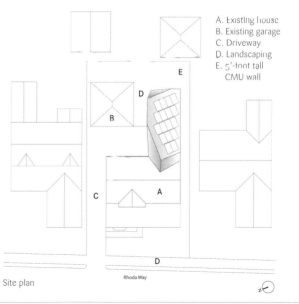

Site plan

Rhoda Way

Section perspectives

Building sections

C

D

E

C

A

B

F

D

A

A. Study
B. Library
C. Bedroom
D. Children's playroom
E. Bridge
F. Photovoltaic panels

The decision to make a two-story addition derived from the need to accommodate the programmatic requirements of the clients, and to position solar panels as high as possible, above the roofline of the existing house and neighboring buildings, maximizing sun exposure.

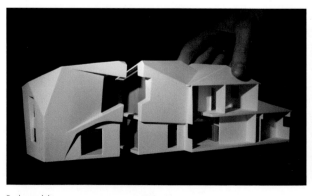

Scale model

The shape of the new addition is sculptural, eye-catching, and far from arbitrary—being determined by the number, the size, and the positioning of the photovoltaic panels that were to be installed on its roof.

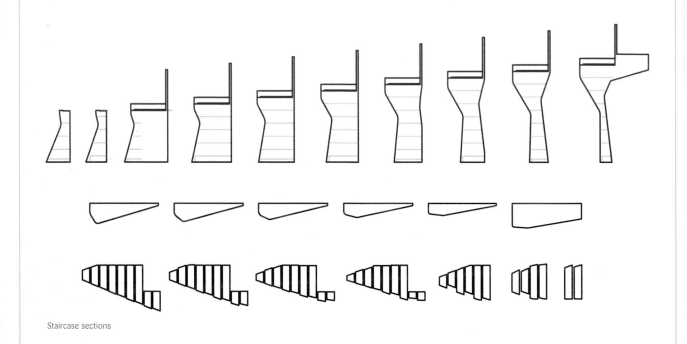

Staircase sections

A new staircase is located between the
addition and existing house. It integrates
the library shelving displaced by the
staircase.

The new stair-shelf hybrid combines the stairs' risers with the bookshelf's vertical supports in a gradient organization that opens toward the main living space.

It is critical to take into account the orientation, size, and number of windows in a room, as they can have a significant impact on energy consumption and comfort.

When artificial lighting is necessary, it is preferable to use energy-efficient technology which will yield substantial energy savings and minimize the emission of related greenhouse gas.

A Considered Something

Statkus Architecture

Northcote, Victoria, Australia

© Matthew Mallet, Ben Starkus

This project is a renovation and extension. The existing house, which had been remodeled by previous owners, was mostly retained, with some reconfiguration and modification of spaces. The project started with a small budget and a small site, but a big brief. Given that the house is for two adults and three children, spaces for everyone formed an important component of the brief. The solution was predicated on the notion that "spaces for everyone" shouldn't necessarily be large rooms, but instead could be undefined, flexible spaces.

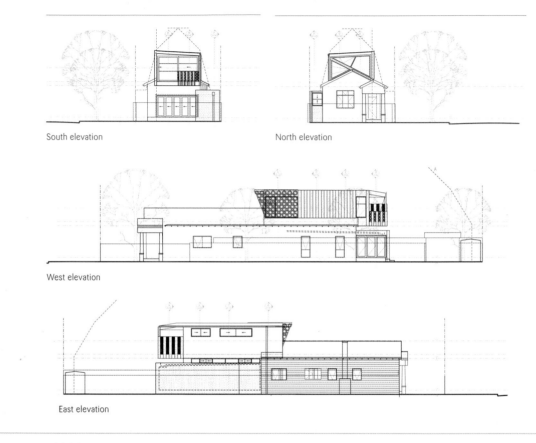

South elevation

North elevation

West elevation

East elevation

This house is on a corner. A bright
orange patterned screen on the upstairs
northwest corner visually addresses
this building by day, contrasting with
the streetscape tones of fence, tree,
and sky.

By night, the screen is inverted, no longer orange, and, with the lights on inside, the openings—dark by day—become light, a lantern effect over the street.

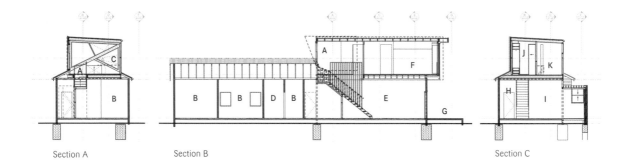

Section A

Section B

Section C

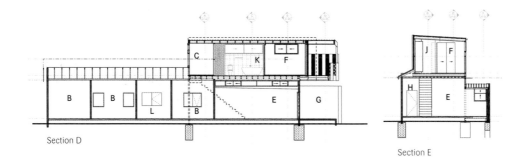

Section D

Section E

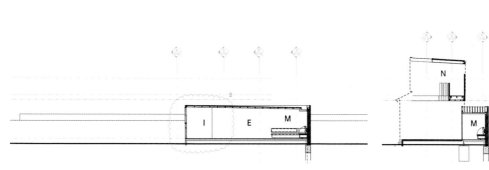

Section F

Section G

A. Stair
B. Bedroom
C. Study
D. Laundry room
E. Living area
F. Master bedroom
G. Deck
H. Dining area
I. Kitchen
J. Dressing area
K. En suite
L. Bathroom
M. Snug
N. Balcony

The new works comprise an extended kitchen, living, and dining area, plus a new "snug" space. A new upstairs extension comprises a study, roof storage access, en suite bathroom, a dressing area, a master bedroom, and a compact balcony.

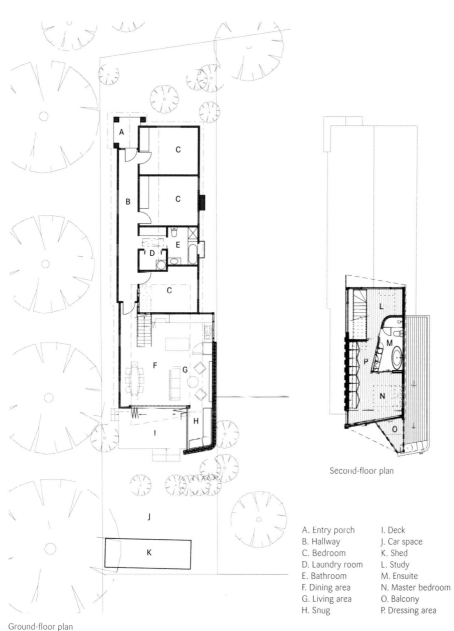

Second-floor plan

Ground-floor plan

A. Entry porch
B. Hallway
C. Bedroom
D. Laundry room
E. Bathroom
F. Dining area
G. Living area
H. Snug

I. Deck
J. Car space
K. Shed
L. Study
M. Ensuite
N. Master bedroom
O. Balcony
P. Dressing area

097

Clerestories are designed to avoid overheating and heat loss. They should be placed according to the orientation of a building to optimize their function.

098

A 6-1/2-foot wide addition to the east boundary extends south beyond the existing rear façade, creating a small "snug" area that experiences warm afternoon sun for a passively warmed and lit space in winter, and a shaded one in summer.

The pattern of the screen is cast upon
the brickwork, tiling, and joinery,
creating constantly changing patterns of
light and shadow.

Transom windows on opposite walls increase the illumination quality by balancing the light. This avoids sharp light and shadow contrasts, and makes for visual comfort.

Ecologia Montréal

Gervais Fortin

Montreal, Quebec, Canada

© Alexandre Parent

This house is the result of a collaborative effort that involved the architect, the owner, and Ecologia Foundation, an environmental organization promoting sustainable development. The design originated with the idea in mind of reducing to a minimum the ecological footprint of the construction by using healthy, local, and little polluting materials. The team demonstrated that it's possible to build an ecological house without sacrificing the contemporary design. All the materials were carefully selected from the most eco-responsible supplier's of the Quebec region.

The stone of the façade, from a local quarry, impresses by its imposing dimensions. A local artisan created hemp and lime walls giving them a rich and velvety aspect. These walls do not contain either gypsum or paint.

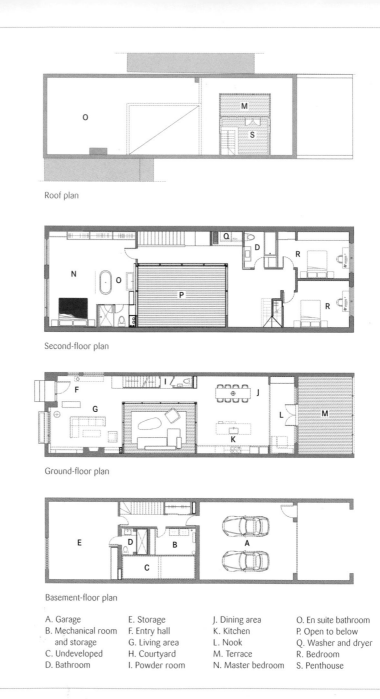

Roof plan

Second-floor plan

Ground-floor plan

Basement-floor plan

A. Garage
B. Mechanical room and storage
C. Undeveloped
D. Bathroom
E. Storage
F. Entry hall
G. Living area
H. Courtyard
I. Powder room
J. Dining area
K. Kitchen
L. Nook
M. Terrace
N. Master bedroom
O. En suite bathroom
P. Open to below
Q. Washer and dryer
R. Bedroom
S. Penthouse

Ecologia Montréal is the first house in Quebec to integrate the BioGeometry™ science, to control electromagnetic fields, to consider the energy of the earth, and to infuse domestic water (in a vortex) which enhances biophotons.

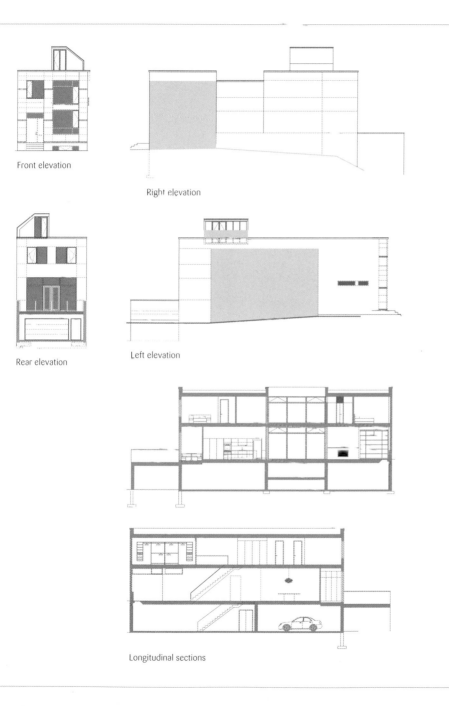

Front elevation

Right elevation

Rear elevation

Left elevation

Longitudinal sections

A combination of exposed beams,
big windows, and an inner courtyard
creates a cozy and modern living space.

099

The panels of the kitchen are made from recycled materials, while all the electrical appliances are among the most durable and the most economical in water and electricity consumption. The faucets include adaptors to reduce the flow of water.

Wide planks of torrefied wood make
the terrace and the inner courtyard
strikingly original living spaces.

100

Ideal in an urban setting, a green roof completes the house. Among the available options, the fiberglass roof was chosen for its waterproofness and its life span of more than one hundred years.

101

The magnificent recycled floors in white ash give the impression of vast and brighter rooms. The radiant floors, combined with a geothermal system, maximize comfort.

102

The indoor furniture was made locally, with materials resistant to daily uses. Made with vegetable-based resin, the bath and vanity of the master bathroom respect eco-friendly values.

Garden Void House

Alva Roy Architects
Toronto, Ontario, Canada
© Tom Arban

This house occupies a corner lot designated as an infill, which in urban planning means an open space that generally can be rededicated to new construction. The two-story house with a basement is set at right angle to a stream, with adequate setbacks. These help avoid obstructing the neighbor's views. Its north- and west-façade setbacks allow natural daylight year-round. Inside, all the floors of the house are organized around a basement garden situated so as to grow vertically through openings in the floor slabs. This design feature reimagines the use of a basement and integrates it with the rest of the house.

Garden Void House is an eye-catching building with powerful straight lines, use of honest materials such as stone and wood, and minute attention to detail.

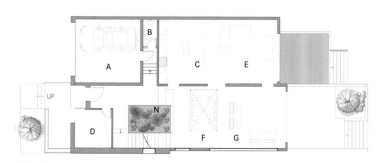

Main-floor plan

Second-floor plan

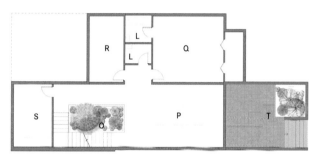

Basement-floor plan

A. Parking
B. Powder room
C. Kitchen
D. Office
E. Family room
F. Dining room
G. Living room

H. Master bedroom
I. Walking closet
J. Master bathroom
K. Bedroom
L. Bathroom
M. Laundry room
N. Open to below

O. Garden
P. Home office
Q. Library
R. Mechanical room
S. Wine cellar and
   cigar room
T. Courtyard

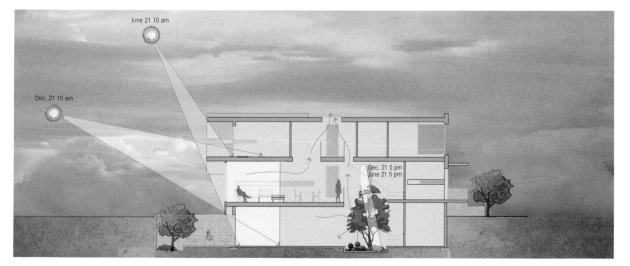

Sun-exposure diagram

A mass-to-void relationship promotes the interconnection among different floors, an effect also enhanced by the basement garden and natural lighting.

103

The garden void and other double-height spaces provide the house with visual and spatial interest, but they are mainly designed as part of the building's energy and lighting efficiency strategy.

104

The days of heat-producing skylights are long past. Improvements include a high haze factor, which permits diffused lighting and offers thermal breaks to optimize energy efficiency.

Clever design and use of materials constrained by budget offered an opportunity to rethink the suburban home. Recycled red brick, raw cement panels, and timber define the overall appearance of this new house exterior. But its most notable feature is its front elevation, which eschews the high fence, in favor of a double garage and upper level, with operable perforated shutters; together, they negotiate the subtle boundary between public and private. Behind lies a singular open-plan volume containing a kitchen, living space, and dining space. A smaller upper level contains two bedrooms, two bathrooms, and a large central void over the dining space, connecting the two volumes.

May Grove Residence

Jackson Clements Burrows Architects

South Yarra, Victoria, Australia

© Peter Clarke

105

Operable shutters perform multiple functions: expose views, control ventilation, admit sunlight, and provide privacy, while engaging with the environment.

106

Thermal mass from the exposed ground-floor slab, coupled with appropriate insulation levels, helps regulate the temperature of an interior space in both summer and winter.

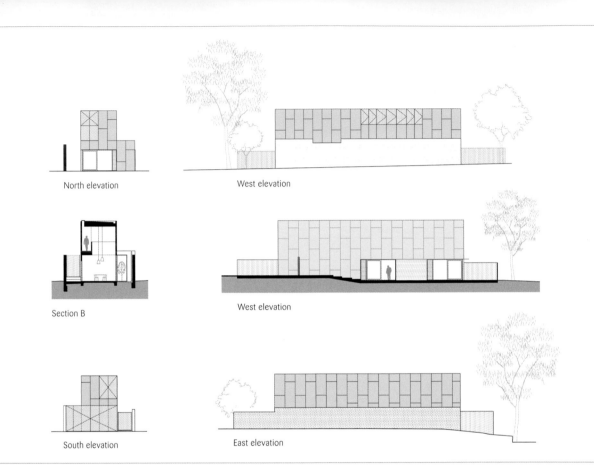

North elevation

West elevation

Section B

West elevation

South elevation

East elevation

107

Heat gain is controlled through double glazing, a steel-blade sunshade over the northern window of the ground-floor façade, and a series of perforated operable shutters over all upper-level windows.

108

A central void acts as a
natural thermal chimney,
where hot air can rise and
then be flushed via effective
cross ventilation.

Ground-floor plan

Second-floor plan

0   1   2,5   5 m

A. Entry deck
B. Entrance/courtyard
C. Powder room
D. Kitchen
E. Laundry room
F. Dining area
G. Courtyard
H. Living area
I. Backyard
J. Service yard

K. Garage
L. Master bedroom
M. Walk-in closet
N. En suite bathroom
O. Hall
P. Bathroom
Q. Bedroom
R. Courtyard below
S. Roof below

The sheer curtain surrounding the void ensures that light and shadow are the main players in an ephemeral internal experience.

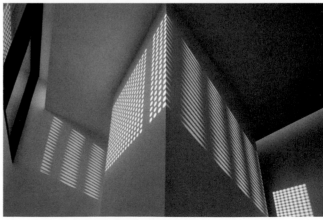

Shotgun Chameleon is inspired both by raised shotgun houses of the U.S. Gulf Coast houses and the versatility of chameleon skin. The design responds to local climate through a front screen that provides a myriad of façade possibilities that can respond to different urban contexts and to a variety of solar and wind exposures. It also emphasizes flexibility and adaptability of interior spaces. Closing the internal stair, this three-bedroom and two-bathroom single-family home can be turned into a duplex for rental, or accommodate a multigenerational family arrangement.

Shotgun Chameleon House

Architect: Zui Ng/ZDES

Houston, Texas, United States

© Paul Hester

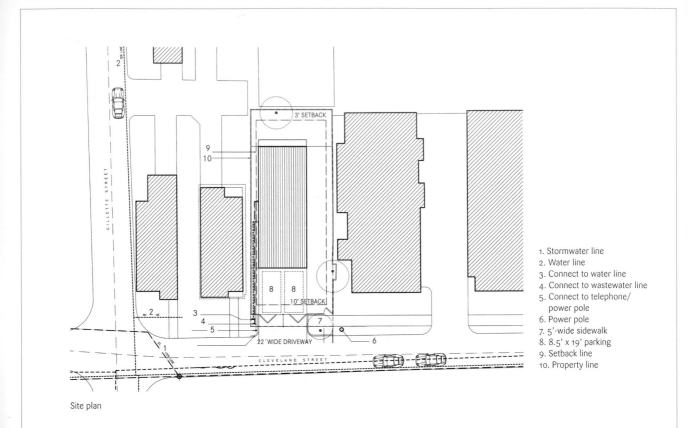

1. Stormwater line
2. Water line
3. Connect to water line
4. Connect to wastewater line
5. Connect to telephone/ power pole
6. Power pole
7. 5'-wide sidewalk
8. 8.5' x 19' parking
9. Setback line
10. Property line

Site plan

109

The angle of the roof was carefully calculated to allow lower winter sunlight to enter the interior spaces, while higher summer sunlight is kept outside.

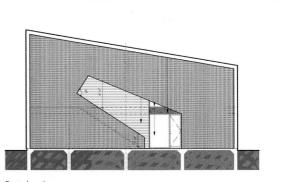

East elevation

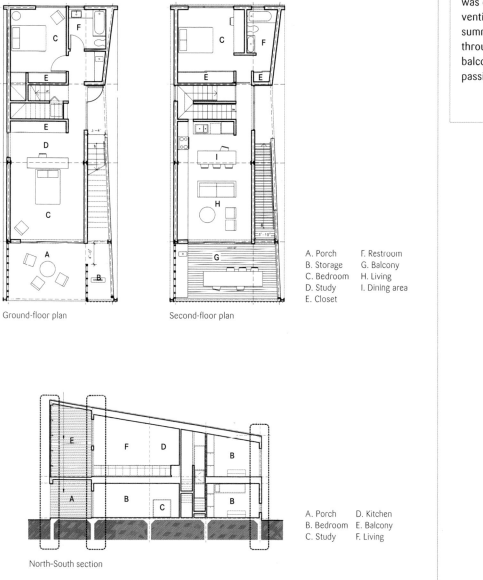

110

This 1,500-square-foot house was designed with cross ventilation in mind. The summer breeze is channeled through the south-facing balcony and porch to passively ventilate the house.

Ground-floor plan

Second-floor plan

A. Porch
B. Storage
C. Bedroom
D. Study
E. Closet

F. Restroom
G. Balcony
H. Living
I. Dining area

North–South section

A. Porch
B. Bedroom
C. Study

D. Kitchen
E. Balcony
F. Living

111

Vertical circulation was planned so that a tenant on the upper floor could use the external staircase, or to connect the two floors in a live-work situation—office space on the ground floor, housing above. This encourages a more sustainable form of home ownership.

112

The wood-slat screens on the sides of the building afford privacy for both the residents and the neighbors, while permitting sunlight and wind to move through the house.

113

Outdoor extensions of interior spaces add flexibility to a home. Protection from the elements (whether permanent or temporary) optimizes their usability.

The design of the house also aims at revisiting and celebrating the idea of balcony and porch living, which is rooted heavily in the vernacular of the Freedmen's Town neighborhood. Opening the sliding-glass doors to the balcony and porch extends the usable space.

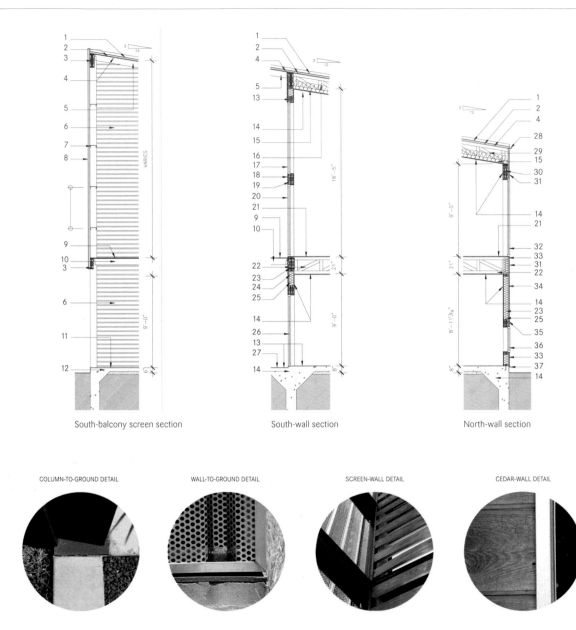

South-balcony screen section

South-wall section

North-wall section

COLUMN-TO-GROUND DETAIL

WALL-TO-GROUND DETAIL

SCREEN-WALL DETAIL

CEDAR-WALL DETAIL

Construction details

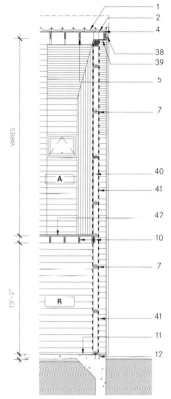

VARIES

13'-2"

A

R

Wood-screen detail

A. Balcony
B. Storage

1. Standing seam-metal roof
2. Vapor barrier underlayment
3. I-beam
4. ¾" plywood decking stamped "CDX-YP"
   with exterior glue
5. 2" x 8" #2 yellow-pinewood roof joists
   at 16" on center
6. 1" x 4" treated wood siding with 1.5"
   gap between planks
7. 8" C girt
8. Corrugated perforated metal
9. 5" x ¾" treated T&G deck
10. 2" x 8" treated yellow pinewood floor
    joists at 16" on center
11. Sealed concrete floor.
    Floor at 1/8" : 12" slope
12. Concrete pear foundation
13. 2" x 6" header
14. ½" birch-plywood ceiling panel
15. R-30 BATT insulation, continuous
16. Roof truss at 16" on center
17. Aluminum window "F"
18. Aluminum to match mullions
19. 2" x 10" header

20. Aluminum sliding-glass door "F"
21. ¾" birch-plywood floor
22. 1'-8"-deep pre-engineered floor truss
23. R-13 BATT insulation continuous
24. Double top plate
25. 2" x 6" #2 yellow-pinewood studs at
    16" on center
26. Aluminum sliding-glass door "A"
27. Floor at 1/8" : 12" slope
28. 3" roof drip edge
29. 1'-6"-deep pre-engineered wood truss
30. 2" x 12" header
31. Corrugated-aluminum wall
32. Insulated aluminum glass window
33. Waterproof membrane
34. ½" OSB sheathing
35. ½" OSB sheathing treated at wall
    below 48"
36. Insulated aluminum glass window
37. Drip edge
38. Aluminum roof trim
39. Treated wood soffit
40. 2" x 6" treated pinewood studs
41. 1" x 4" treated pinewood slat alternate
    pattern
42. 2" x 4" treated pine deck

A privacy fence is one of the most common design solutions to block a view. It can also double as a screen for sun protection. Regardless of the purpose, the fence or screen of Shotgun Chameleon House is an integral element of the building's design.

114

Optimizing the functional relationship between program and space, providing such spaces with flexible use, and minimizing circulation areas all contribute to most efficient possible use of space and materials.

115

The choice of renewable wood material, high-efficiency mechanical equipment (such as mini split AC units and a tankless water heater), dual-flush toilet, LED lighting, foam insulation, and low-e insulated windows drastically reduces energy consumption.

A double-height window in the living room frames an ever-evolving urban view to the south, while taking in abundant filtered light.

A large opening in the bedroom frames the views of the garden to the north. The placement of the room at the rear of the house responds to the need for privacy. At the same time, it leaves the southern end of the house to the living spaces, which benefit from a sunnier exposure.

The Mosman Bay House explores two contrasting spatial experiences. One is dynamic and fluid, the other passive and contemplative; one focuses on the distant views to the river and city; the other is embedded within the garden. These contrasting qualities respond to the programmatic requirements of communal and private spaces: on one hand, living, dining, and cooking areas; and on the other, rooms for sleeping, working, and bathing. In a reference to the Eames's *Powers of Ten*, the design team explored multiple scales of relating to the site, fluctuating between distant views and engagement with the garden and the pool.

Mosman Bay House

Iredale Pedersen Hook

Perth, Western Australia, Australia

© Peter Benetts

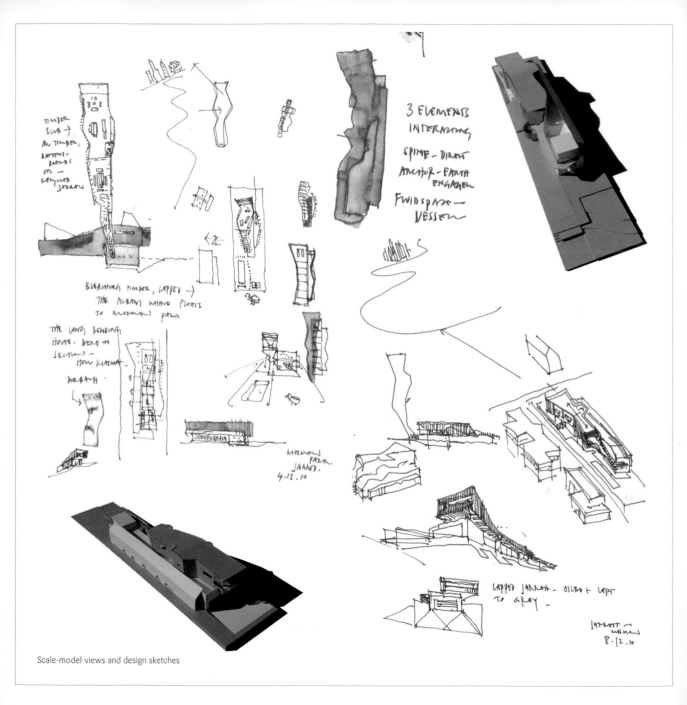

Scale-model views and design sketches

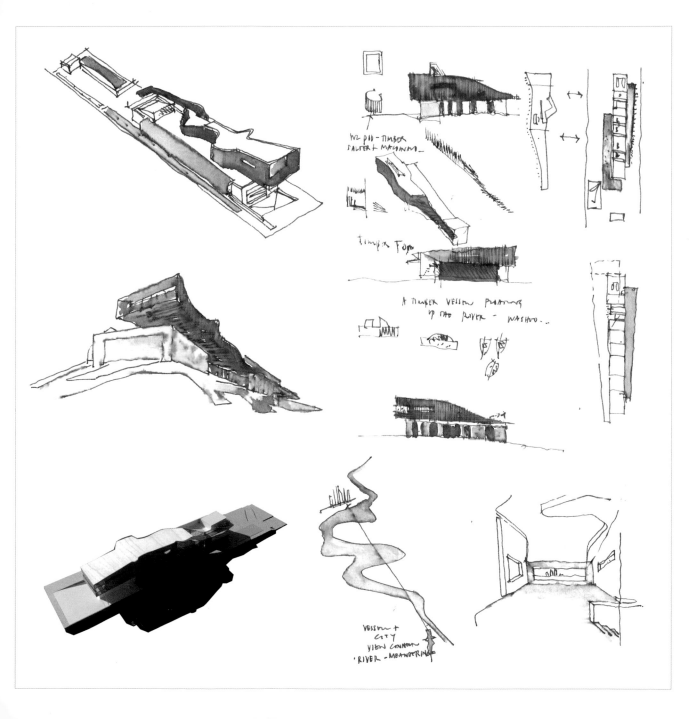

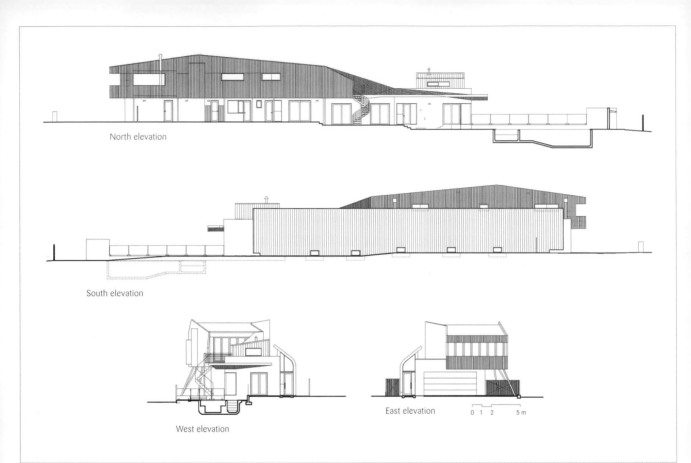

North elevation

South elevation

West elevation

East elevation

0 1 2   5 m

116

The house is on a long and narrow site in an east–west orientation. This greatly influenced the house's environmental design of the house, as it enables the interior spaces to be configured for optimal northern passive heat gain in winter.

Perspective view

Section A

Section C

Section B

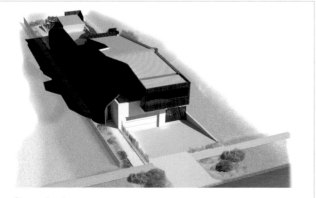

Perspective view

The roof detailing continues the meandering profile and incorporates Pittsburgh seams developed in close consultation with the builder and roofing contractor. While steel might not be the most obvious material for this project it is specifically designed and adapted to be high performing environmentally and structurally.

The materials chosen for the exterior
have a tactile quality and are designed
to weather naturally. The upper floor—
clad in recycled and lapped Jarrah—is
conceived as a vessel that meanders
above the ground floor of white
sand-rendered walls. It expresses the
dynamism of the activities that take
place in the interior.

The upper level shifts further north to create a continuous veranda protecting ground-level spaces from summer sun, while allowing the southern neighbor to still enjoy winter sun.

117

A pergola undulates in a
dialogue with a meandering
river in the vicinity. Supported
by a steel tube and a
structural flat-bar fascia,
it protects the lower-level
glazing from summer sun.

118

The south-facing sculptured wall was modeled to allow north-facing light and heat gain. It is also specifically shaped to facilitate southwestern wind drafts that blow over cooling ponds and into the house via low-level windows.

A hidden space with gas fire pit and flowing recycled water allows one to "drift" on the edge of the property.

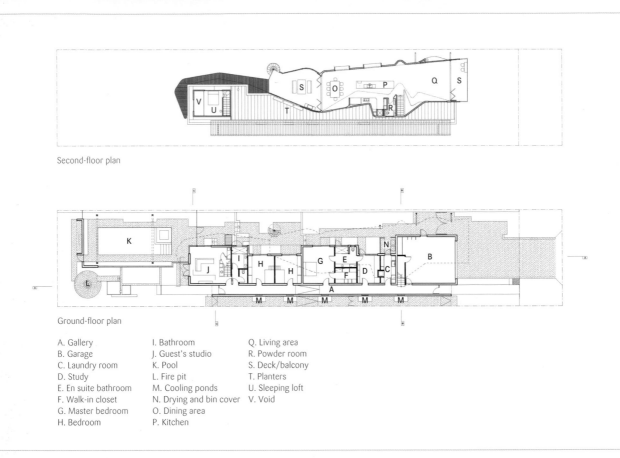

Second-floor plan

Ground-floor plan

A. Gallery
B. Garage
C. Laundry room
D. Study
E. En suite bathroom
F. Walk-in closet
G. Master bedroom
H. Bedroom

I. Bathroom
J. Guest's studio
K. Pool
L. Fire pit
M. Cooling ponds
N. Drying and bin cover
O. Dining area
P. Kitchen

Q. Living area
R. Powder room
S. Deck/balcony
T. Planters
U. Sleeping loft
V. Void

The house extends along the east-west axis of the site, the lower-level spaces all facing north onto intimate and personal gardens, collecting winter sun and passive heat gain.

119

A long, narrow space open at both ends extends along the entire length of the house, admitting the southwestern winds into the house. A series of small cooling ponds are placed adjacent to ground-level awning windows.

120

The ground-level spaces can be compartmentalized to allow easy heating and cooling and individual control. Fans are provided to the ground-level spaces for additional cooling. There is no air conditioning in these spaces.

Ferns create a secluded and lush natural screen for the study and bathrooms on the ground floor. The materials chosen for the bathroom reflect green light into the study and bathing areas.

The Mosman Bay House exploits the
potential of lighting to enhance the
formal qualities of the design. Lighting
is critical to the unfolding of the spatial
experience, which is sometimes subtle,
sometimes overstated.

121

Inside, dark floors were chosen for their ability to absorb the heat of solar rays in winter, while light-colored materials were selected for the roof and exterior masonry walls to reduce heat gain.

The veranda and profile of the upper level were shaped by solar modeling that assessed winter sun penetration to lower levels and by considering of the functional requirements of the upper level.

Malvern House

Jost Architects

Malvern, Victoria, Australia

© Fraser Marsden

This project involved a small, interwar, semidetached house that, despite the local council's Heritage B grading, appeared to have very few significant architectural features. From the outset, this posed challenges to achieving the client's enthusiastic brief. The planning restraints meant that a two-level rear extension was an option: the client's brief had to be slightly condensed and adapted, while retaining all the functional needs. An alteration and an addition made in the '80s were removed to make room for the new design.

North elevation

South elevation

East elevation

West elevation

- - - - - Boundary

▨ Adjoining building

The entry and beginning of the new section is unassuming, recessed from the front façade. This satisfied the heritage requirements of keeping the original white cement bagged brick building intact. The new section clearly defines the location of the entrance with a new dark-burnt-ash timber wall.

404 Malvern House

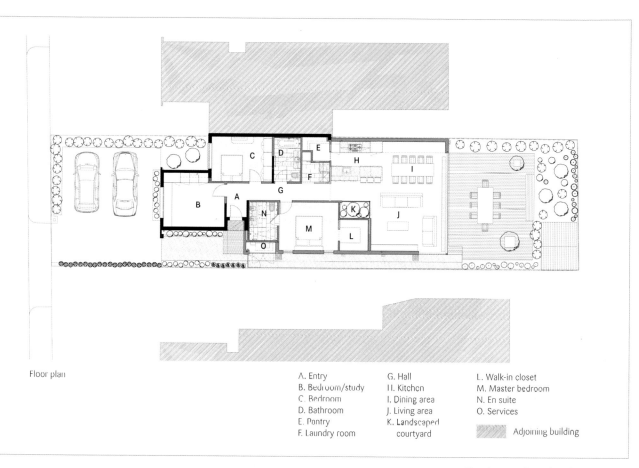

Floor plan

A. Entry
B. Bedroom/study
C. Bedroom
D. Bathroom
E. Pantry
F. Laundry room

G. Hall
H. Kitchen
I. Dining area
J. Living area
K. Landscaped
courtyard

L. Walk-in closet
M. Master bedroom
N. En suite
O. Services

░░░░░ Adjoining building

The plan is traditional, with rooms accessible from a central corridor leading to the rear dining and living area, where the ceiling rakes up to a substantial height. This transition creates a dramatic effect in an otherwise modestly sized home.

122

Extending a living area outdoors space can increase the usable square footage of a home, and can create an all-year-round oasis rather than a seasonal spot, depending on the climate.

A view of to the back garden was imperative to the client's brief. With a higher-than-usual ceiling and double-stacking, glazed steel-framed sliding doors, an unimpeded view was achieved. The impression when the glass doors to the garden are open, is that, standing at the entry, there is no enclosed space beyond the corridor.

Highlight windows that provide controlled northern sunlight complement the generous proportions of the living area. The double-stacking, full-height doors connect the space to the spotted-gum deck and dense perimeter landscaping.

123

An internal courtyard lends the kitchen area a peaceful point of interest, as well as providing it with light and ventilation.

124

The detail is careful and clean, but controlled to sit within the budget. Sustainable applications include durable materials such as thermally modified timber cladding, double-glazed steel windows and sliding doors, and the use of zoned hydronic heating.

S11 House

DrTanLM Architect

Selangor, Malaysia
© H. Lin Ho

An existing house on the site, built in the early 1960s, and grown dilapidated over the years. The site also included five significant trees: three very old frangipanis, a large star fruit, and a coconut palm tree. These trees were retained, and the designers were determined to take full advantage of great shading benefits they offered. The new landscaping was conceived with sustainability in mind, species were chosen for their low-maintenance qualities and their suitability for the Malaysian climate. S11 House was designed to achieve the highest-level Platinum rating of Malaysia's Green Building Index (GBI).

125

Rainwater-harvesting systems are composed of three parts: a roof (or other catchment surface), the piping that channels the water, and storage tanks. The water collected in tanks is generally used for toilet flushing, gardening, and other gray-water needs.

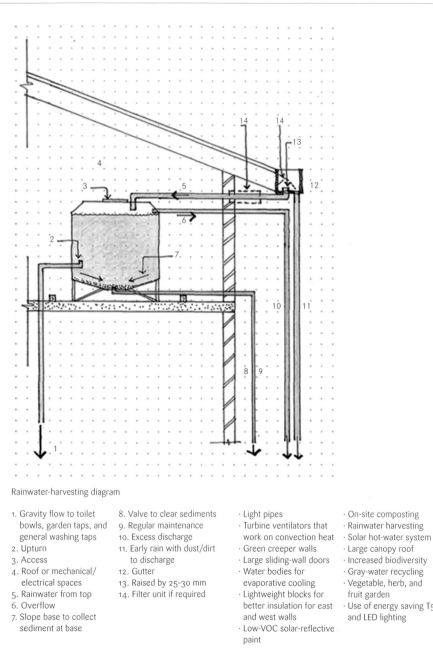

Rainwater-harvesting diagram

1. Gravity flow to toilet bowls, garden taps, and general washing taps
2. Upturn
3. Access
4. Roof or mechanical/electrical spaces
5. Rainwater from top
6. Overflow
7. Slope base to collect sediment at base
8. Valve to clear sediments
9. Regular maintenance
10. Excess discharge
11. Early rain with dust/dirt to discharge
12. Gutter
13. Raised by 25–30 mm
14. Filter unit if required

· Light pipes
· Turbine ventilators that work on convection heat
· Green creeper walls
· Large sliding-wall doors
· Water bodies for evaporative cooling
· Lightweight blocks for better insulation for east and west walls
· Low-VOC solar-reflective paint

· On-site composting
· Rainwater harvesting
· Solar hot-water system
· Large canopy roof
· Increased biodiversity
· Gray-water recycling
· Vegetable, herb, and fruit garden
· Use of energy saving T5 and LED lighting

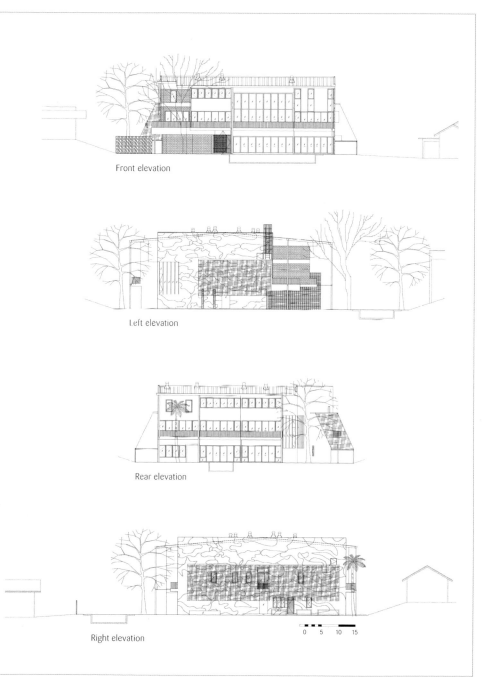

Front elevation

Left elevation

Rear elevation

Right elevation

0 5 10 15

Much of the debris from the demolished old house was reused. Crushed-concrete roof tiles became gravel fill; clay bricks were cleaned and reused for feature walls; roofing wood sheathing was used for formwork, strutting, and propping; and steel was sold to steelyards.

126

The east and west walls have no significant openings and are built with highly insulated lightweight concrete blocks finished in heat-reflecting paint, featuring a camouflage pattern. A steel trellis for climbers in front of these walls add a further layer of insulation.

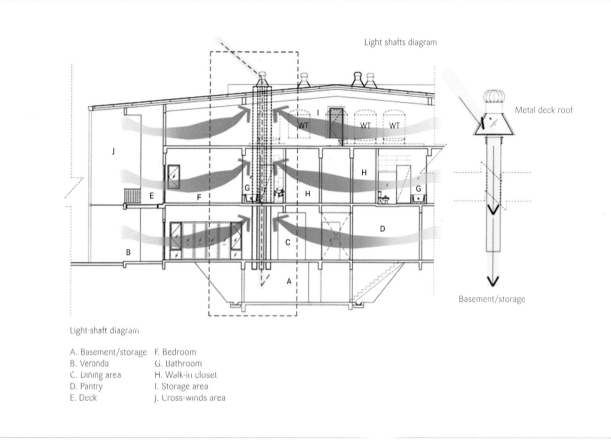

Light shafts diagram

Metal deck roof

WT   WT   WT

J

H

E   F   G   H   G

B   C   D

A

Basement/storage

Light-shaft diagram

A. Basement/storage   F. Bedroom
B. Veranda   G. Bathroom
C. Dining area   H. Walk-in closet
D. Pantry   I. Storage area
E. Deck   J. Cross-winds area

127

A wind turbine, combined with a steel-framed glazed pyramid, provides the house with "stack effect" ventilation and light pipes. These turbines are driven both by wind, as well as by convection, which happens when the air within the glass pyramids heats up and rises.

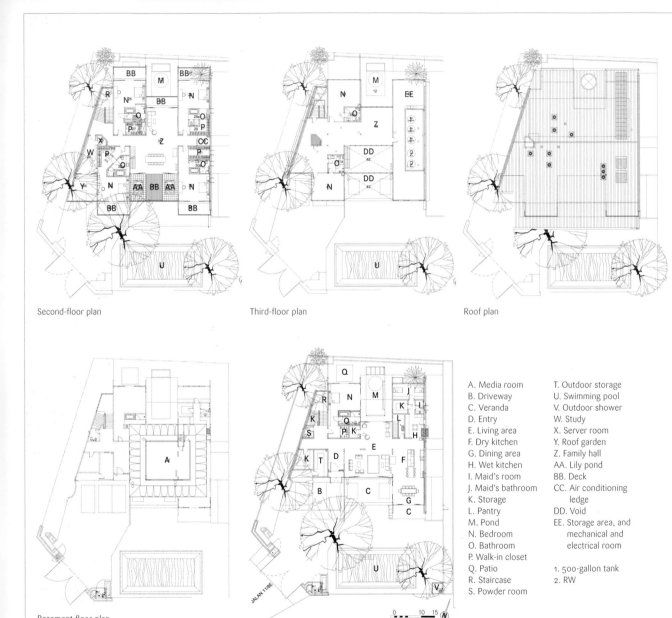

Second-floor plan

Third-floor plan

Roof plan

Basement-floor plan

Ground-floor plan

JALAN 11/8E

0   10   15   N

A. Media room
B. Driveway
C. Veranda
D. Entry
E. Living area
F. Dry kitchen
G. Dining area
H. Wet kitchen
I. Maid's room
J. Maid's bathroom
K. Storage
L. Pantry
M. Pond
N. Bedroom
O. Bathroom
P. Walk-in closet
Q. Patio
R. Staircase
S. Powder room

T. Outdoor storage
U. Swimming pool
V. Outdoor shower
W. Study
X. Server room
Y. Roof garden
Z. Family hall
AA. Lily pond
BB. Deck
CC. Air conditioning
    ledge
DD. Void
EE. Storage area, and
    mechanical and
    electrical room

1. 500-gallon tank
2. RW

128

The house boasts exposed formed concrete walls and ceilings, plaster walls, and red clay brickwork. The ground floor decking is made of old recycled chengal, while the wood flooring and upper decks are all Forest Stewardship Council (FSC) certified.

129

LED lighting, with innovative features such as LED T5 and LED T8 tubes, flexible lighting and down lighting, is the next-generation technology. It features higher energy efficiency than CFLs and fluorescents, lower power usage, and longer lifetimes.

The modular bookshelves are made from recycled plywood scraps. Also, all other joinery has low VOC content, and water-based glue was used in its assembly.

130

Natural ventilation can be achieved through low and high openings within a room, or by connecting various separate spaces to a vertical air path such a staircase or an atrium.

The 23-foot-high sliding-glass walls of the double-height family room on the second floor facilitate cross ventilation.

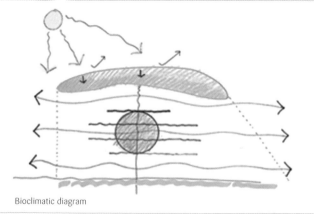

Bioclimatic diagram

131

The roof, along with the east and west camouflage walls, provides enough insulation to minimize heat gain. The trees form a screen for the living areas, while the koi pond and swimming pool provide evaporative cooling for the entire house.

Clay Roof House

DrTanLM Architect
Selangor, Malaysia
© H. Lin Ho

Clay Roof House is located on a small lot, the former site of a dilapidated house. Inspection of the old house had revealed good-quality Indian clay roof tiles that were still robust and thus offered repurposing opportunities. This unexpected find gave the house a unique character and set the tone for the rest of the design, which implemented recycled and raw materials. There is a touch of purism in the raw walls and in the use of building materials in their natural form, a breath of minimalism in the simple lines, unornamented motifs, and open spaces.

132

Direct exposure to the afternoon sun was an issue to which the clay roof tiles offered an ingenious solution: they act as a vertical screen for the west-facing façade.

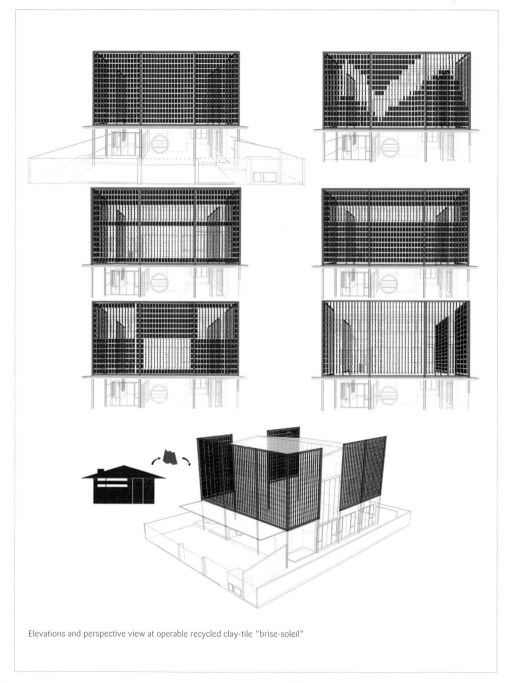

The clay tile and lattice brickwork screens transform the house into an insulated and well-ventilated cube, comprising volumes of spaces with unique spatial and lighting qualities.

Elevations and perspective view at operable recycled clay-tile "brise-soleil"

The roof tiles were carefully removed, stored, and reused. Vertical steel rods were designed to hold the clay tiles, while allowing free movement.

The clay-tile screens reduce solar gain through windows and glass doors. From an aesthetic standpoint, the tiles glow with a warm, orange color during the day, and filter interior lighting at night, creating an eye-catching pattern.

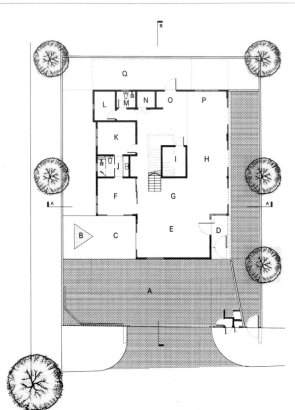

Ground-floor plan

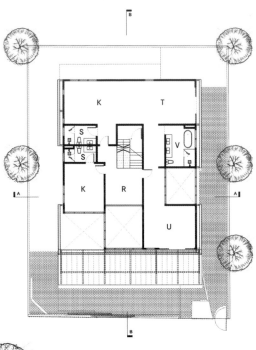

Second-floor plan

A. Carport
B. Pond
C. Deck
D. Entry
E. Living area
F. Study
G. Piano room
H. Dining area
I. Storage
J. Powder room
K. Bedroom

L. Maid's room
M. Maid's bathroom
N. Pantry
O. Wet kitchen
P. Dry kitchen
Q. Laundry and yard
R. Foyer
S. Bathroom
T. TV area
U. Master bedroom
V. Master bathroom

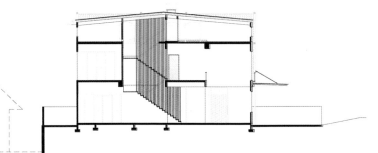

Section B

133

The recycling of materials is part of sustainable design. Reuse of construction materials such as brick or steel allows for the distribution of their environmental impact over an extended period of time.

134

Brick masonry walls used in sustainable design can provide structure, finish, acoustic and thermal comfort, fire resistance, and durability. Among finishing materials, it is among the lowest in VOCs.

Air movement is the most important element in passive cooling. Choose ceiling fans over evaporative coolers and air conditioners to achieve energy efficiency and minimize costs.

Ceiling fans come in a variety of materials—mainly wood, molded plastic, and steel; the right choice depends on the location. For instance, in a coastal environment, choose a fan with wood blades—steel would corrode.

The folded-steel staircase enhances
the industrial character of the house,
harmonizing with the raw materials used
throughout.

Vali Homes Infill
Prototype II

coLAB studio

Phoenix, Arizona, United States

© Bill Timmerman,
  Aaron Rothman

This house responds to the need for the creation of affordable and sustainable housing for infill lots across metropolitan Phoenix. Working with Vali Homes, a developer and sustainability consultant, and 180 Degrees, a design-build company, coLAB studio has engaged in studying various structures, methods, and materials for building eco-friendly homes. These homes are meant as contemporary, site-specific, and sustainable equivalents of the "case study" houses of the 1950s and '60s. Prototype II was built to passive house standards—though not certified. But the design approach had a positive impact on the neighborhood, driving up property values.

The plan is simple, attempting to optimize efficiency, while maximizing the 40-foot width of the lot, ensuring that the home will fit on any typical lot in Phoenix. The nearly square shape minimizes exterior surface area and maximizes energy efficiency.

137

Dimensions are based on the use of full sheets of plywood sheathing, metal cladding, and gypsum board. Keeping the mechanical room at the center and aligning the bathrooms and mechanical room allows for short duct runs, which results in plumbing efficiency.

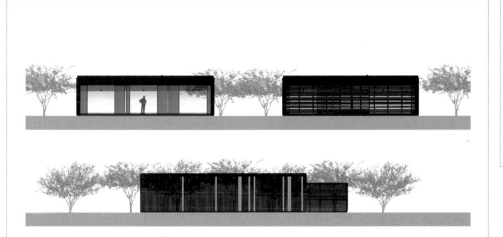

Elevations

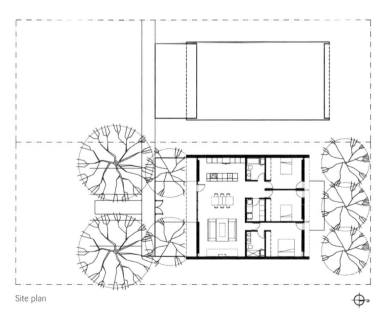

Site plan

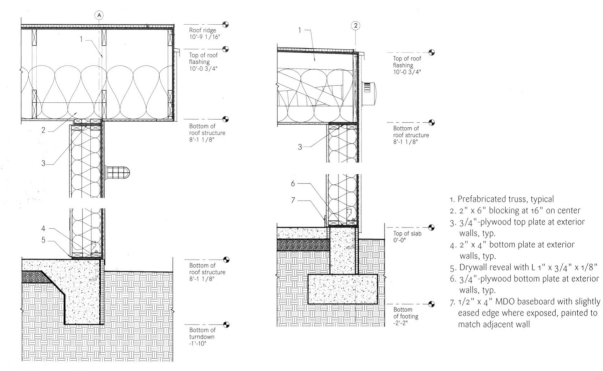

Roof ridge
10'-9 1/16"

Top of roof
flashing
10'-0 3/4"

Bottom of
roof structure
8'-1 1/8"

Top of roof
flashing
10'-0 3/4"

Bottom of
roof structure
8'-1 1/8"

Bottom of
roof structure
8'-1 1/8"

Bottom of
turndown
-1'-10"

Top of slab
0'-0"

Bottom
of footing
-2'-2"

1. Prefabricated truss, typical
2. 2" x 6" blocking at 16" on center
3. 3/4"-plywood top plate at exterior
   walls, typ.
4. 2" x 4" bottom plate at exterior
   walls, typ.
5. Drywall reveal with L 1" x 3/4" x 1/8"
6. 3/4"-plywood bottom plate at exterior
   walls, typ.
7. 1/2" x 4" MDO baseboard with slightly
   eased edge where exposed, painted to
   match adjacent wall

Wall section details

138

A high-performance window
or door can prevent
infiltration (inadvertent
leakage of air and
condensation) and can offer
ultraviolet protection from the
unwanted effects of fading.

The variable spacing of the steel slats of the courtyard fence offers a comfortable balance of openness and privacy, allowing the courtyard to become an outdoor extension of the living area.

139

The 1,680-square-foot house will use around 5,000 kWh (about $450 worth) of electricity per year. A planned 3-kW solar photovoltaic power collection system will offset 100 percent of the annual energy use.

140

The ultimate sustainable kitchen is one that promotes an eco-friendly lifestyle and includes energy-efficient appliances, low-flow faucets, and reflective surfaces that can reduce the need for electrical lighting during the day.

141

High-performance, energy-efficient windows can make a huge impact on the energy consumption of a home. Various types of glazing and specialized transparent coatings help to minimize heat loss and air leakage.

House T

Studio arquitectos

Tulum, Quintana Roo, Mexico
© Pablo Garcia Figueroa

House T is a private residence composed of three vacation
studios. The client, a New York fashion designer, wanted a
space set amidst the vibrant textures and colors of a Caribbean
paradise, and, most important, one adapted to the tropical
framework. The concept "coming from a city—New York—to
the Tropical Caribbean—Tulum" is expressed through the
juxtaposition of polished cement and lush vegetation.
The client's involvement in the design insured a personalized
house organized around a distinctive geometry and a striking
combination of materials that visually play on the "T" brand name.

142

The effort to minimize the impact of the building on the site entailed the preservation of many of the existing trees, which in turn, are integrated into the design of the house.

The integration of natural elements
into the design of the house results
in a composition of shapes, rhythms,
and textures, catching the spectator by
surprise at every turn of a corner.

The formed-concrete shell is filled in with glass panels, most of which slide open to seamlessly connect interior and exterior spaces, and enhance the clarity of the building's structure.

143

The concrete industry is making advances in reducing energy consumption and the emission of greenhouse gas. One of concrete's environmental benefits is its high thermal mass, which reduce energy usage.

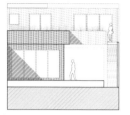

Front elevation

Back elevation

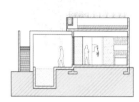

Section T01

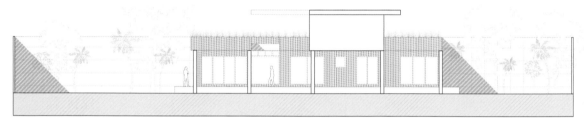

Side elevation

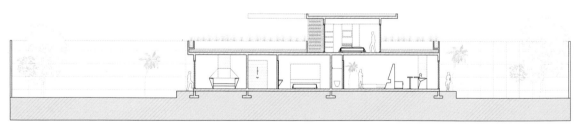

Section L01

0   1   2,5   5 m

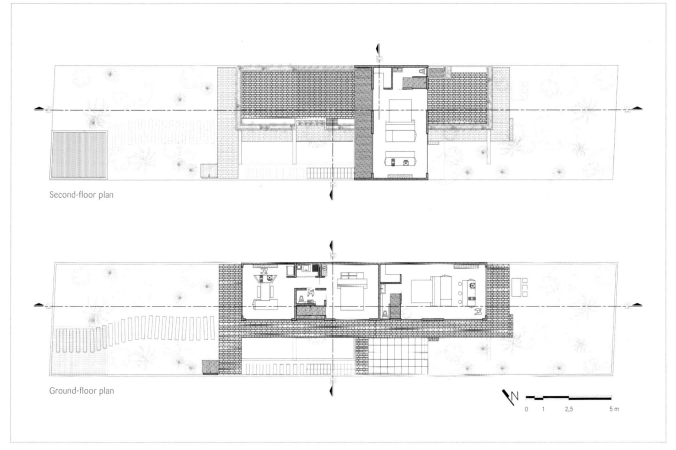

Second-floor plan

Ground-floor plan

N
0   1   2,5   5 m

144

The house boasts a feeling
of lightness, mainly achieved
through the perpendicular
stacking of the two floors.
This orthogonal positioning
generates a series of outdoor
spaces, some open to the
elements, others protected
under deep cantilevers.

Exposed raw materials are used throughout the house, creating a seamless continuity between interior and exterior spaces.

In line with the design concept of
the project—urban dwelling meets
Caribbean paradise—the modularity of
the concrete staircase contrasts with
the organic forms found in the garden.

Mosaic floor and wall tile and a formed concrete vanity lend this bathroom a sophisticated urban appeal in keeping with the concept of the design.

Raw House sits on a long and narrow site, an urban scrap resulting from a subdivided family plot. The area of 21 x 90 feet, with a west façade, presented a challenging opportunity to explore creative design solutions that would make the most of the available space. The house rises three levels with generously proportioned and light-filled interior spaces. The design approach focuses on sustainable strategies, including passive cooling and heating, as well as the use of natural, common, and readily available materials, for which the project is named. Materials are left bare and exposed for a better appreciation of their intrinsic beauty.

Raw House

Taller Estilo Arquitectura
Mérida, Mexico
© David Cervera

145

The pool is strategically located close to the back wall of the house. It can cool the air before it enters the house through the tall glass doors, guided by the two side walls.

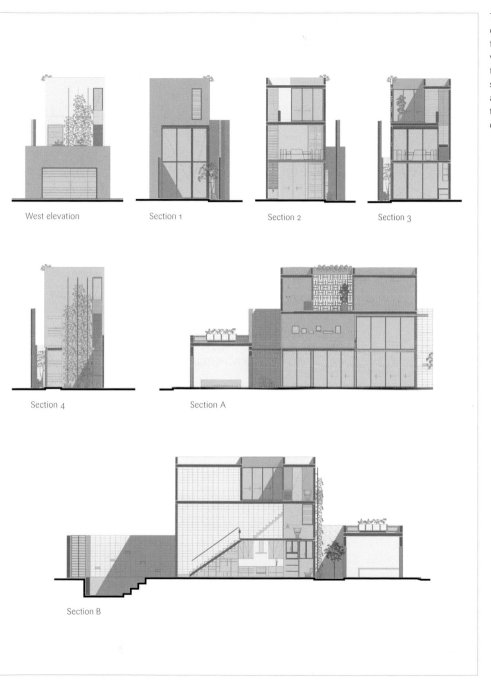

West elevation

Section 1

Section 2

Section 3

Section 4

Section A

Section B

The configuration of the spaces confronts the issues of sunlight entering from west and the need for cross ventilation throughout. The key was the creation of a solid volume that screens off the light from the west, and a 2-1/2-foot-wide light well along the north wall that acts as a thermal chimney.

146

The limited and narrow proportions of the site guided the design of the house, which resulted in a slim, three-level structure. The openings at the front and back of the house are maximized to channel air drafts through its interior.

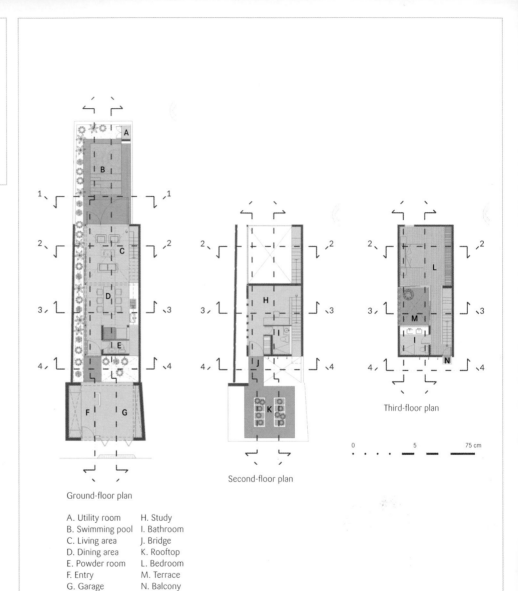

Ground-floor plan

Second-floor plan

Third-floor plan

0 ···· 5 ▬▬ 75 cm

A. Utility room
B. Swimming pool
C. Living area
D. Dining area
E. Powder room
F. Entry
G. Garage
H. Study
I. Bathroom
J. Bridge
K. Rooftop
L. Bedroom
M. Terrace
N. Balcony

147

Interior courtyards create intermediate microclimates between the outdoors and the interior of a building. These semi-outdoor spaces combine climate, nature, and space to achieve thermal comfort.

148

The narrow light well along the north side is a source of natural light. It also acts as a thermal chimney when the sliding doors are open. This energy-efficient design element is used to regulate the temperature of a space, as well as to provide ventilation.

Tucked under the second-level floor slab, the kitchen is compact and space efficient, featuring a full wall of built-in cabinets. The lowered ceiling allows for task lighting above the dining table.

High ceilings and full-height pivot doors that open up the living area to the east patio, with its pool, make the interior appear larger than it actually is.

Concrete block, glass, and steel are showcased in their natural condition. Together, they define the aesthetic character of the home. The ordinary concrete masonry unit, so common in the area, is a modular reference that sets the tone for the design of the entire house.

149

Floors and woodwork elements—mostly recycled from old doors—increase the sound absorption capacity of the building, mainly built of concrete, steel, and glass. Unlike wood, these materials reflect sound more than they absorb it.

150

A central terrace on the top floor and a small balcony on the west façade provide the bedroom with cross ventilation. Openings located on opposite sides of a space will effectively draw air through it.

DIRECTORY

Adam Knibb Architects
Winchester, Hampshire,
United Kingdom
www.adamknibbarchitects.com

AGATHOM Co.
Toronto, Ontario, Canada
https://agathom.com

Alva Roy Architects
Toronto, Ontario, Canada
www.alvaroy.ca

AssemblageSTUDIO
Las Vegas, Nevada, United States
www.assemblagestudio.com

Bates Masi + Architects
East Hampton and New York,
New York, United States
http://batesmasi.com

Bercy Chen Studio
Austin, Texas, and Los Angeles,
California, United States
Taipei, Taiwan, China
Mexico City, Mexico
http://bcarc.com

Caramel Architekten
Linz, Austria
www.caramel.at

Chevallier Architectes
Chamonix Mont-Blanc, France
http://chevallier-architectes.fr

coLAB
Tempe, Arizona, United States
www.colabstudio.com

DrTanLM Architect
Selangor, Malaysia
www.drtanlokemun.com

Dunn & Hillam Architects
Botany, New South Wales, Australia
http://dunnhillam.com.au

DUST
Tucson, Arizona, United States
www.dustdb.com

Fivedot
Seattle, Washington, United States
www.fivedotdesignbuild.com

GITC
Santiago, Chile
www.gitc.cl

Gervais Fortin
Montréal, Québec, Canada
www.gervaisfortin.com

iredale pedersen hook
Melbourne, Victoria, and Perth,
Western Australia, Australia
http://iredalepedersenhook.com

**Jackson Clements Burrows
Architects**
Melbourne, Victoria, Australia
www.jcba.com.au

John Grable Architects
San Antonio, Texas, United States
http://www.johngrable.com

Jost Architects
St Kilda, Victoria, Australia
http://jostarchitects.com

Julie Firkin Architects
Abbotsford, Victoria, Australia
www.j-f-a.com.au

Matt Fajkus Architecture
Austin, Texas, United States
www.mfarchitecture.com

MU Architecture
Montréal, Québec, Canada
www.architecture-mu.com

Officina29 Architetti
Sassari, Sardinia, Italy
www.officina29architetti.com

Open Source Architecture
Los Angeles, California, United States
www.o-s-a.com

Pierre Cabana Architecte
Magog, Quebec, Canada
architecte@cabanapierre.ca

Statkus Architecture
Northcote, Victoria, Australia
www.statkusarchitecture.com.au

Stelle Lomont Rouhani Architects
Bridgehampton, New York,
United States
www.stelleco.com

Studio Arquitectos
Tulum, Quintana Roo, Mexico
www.studioarqs.com.mx

Taller Estilo Arquitectura
Mérida, Yucatán, Mexico
www.tallerestiloarquitectura.com

Turnbull Grifin Haesloop Architects
San Francisco, California, United States
www.tgharchitects.com

UNStudio
Amsterdam, The Netherlands
Shanghai, China
Hong Kong, SAR of China
www.unstudio.com

Ward + Blake Architects
Jackson, Wyoming, United States
http://wardblakearchitects.com

ZeroEnergy Design
Boston and Orleans, Massachusetts,
United States
http://zeroenergy.com

ZDES
Houston, Texas, United States
http://zdes.webs.com